America's First City

St. Augustine's Historic Neighborhoods

by

Karen Harvey

Tailored Tours Publications, Inc.
Box 22861
Lake Buena Vista, FL 32830

America's First City

is dedicated to

The people of St. Augustine
whose love of the Ancient City
I sincerely share

Other Books by Karen Harvey

Alexandria, Virginia: A Pictorial History
Flagler Hospital "A Gift for Life"
St. Augustine and St. Johns County: A Pictorial History

First Edition

ISBN: 0–9631241–2–9

Library of Congress Catalog Card Number: 92-061745

Cover Design:
Success by Design, Inc.

Foreword

St. Augustine's Historic Eras

First Spanish Period	1565–1763
British Decades	1763–1784
Second Spanish Regime	1784–1821
Territorial Days	1821–1845
Early Statehood	1845–1888
Flagler Golden Era	1888–1914
Twentieth Century	1914–present

The preservation of historic buildings logically begins with their identification and description. That is accomplished by conducting a historical survey, the process of locating, describing, and documenting the buildings, objects, archaeological materials, and other physical remains of the past that invest a particular community. The contents of this book grew out of the survey of historical resources in the City of St. Augustine that was conducted under the auspices of the Historic St. Augustine Preservation Board from 1978 through 1981.

Historic preservation did not begin in St. Augustine with that survey, however. Indeed, efforts to preserve the distinctive resources found in the community, a small place intensively occupied for more than four centuries by European settlers and their descendants and by Indian peoples for thousands of years before that, have been going on in a haphazard way for about a century and in an organized fashion since the mid–1930s.

No professional or systematic survey of the city's neighborhoods has previously been attempted. The reason for that may be attributed to America's changing perception of historic preservation, which has since the 1960s experienced a metamorphosis in popularity and nature. Before then, preservation focused on protecting only the obviously distinctive buildings or resources in the community that possessed historical value. In the years since the end of World War II, the face of America has changed dramatically. Whole neighborhoods and streets lined with the graceful

1996

APR

architecture of the past have disappeared, replaced too often by mass–produced buildings that exhibit neither style or attractiveness. People concerned about the architectural heritage of the country came to realize that historic preservation should concentrate not merely upon individual buildings, but upon whole neighborhoods.

In St. Augustine, historic preservation, which involved the collaborative efforts of city, county, state, and private entities, had concerned itself essentially with preserving the colonial remnants found within the historic Walled City. Few Colonial Period buildings remained in the 1960s, perhaps only three dozen in all, many of them are highly altered from their original appearance. The architectural legacy of the post–Colonial Period, that time since 1821 had, in the meantime, been largely ignored. The 1978–81 survey for the first time documented the historic resources embracing all of St. Augustine's remarkable past.

Parts of the city's 19th century architectural legacy were, of course, hard to ignore. The monumental hotels which Henry Morrison Flagler constructed in the 1880s in his hope of creating a "southern Newport" enjoyed national recognition for their important place in architectural history. Less obvious were the houses that developed around them and which historically and architecturally complemented the majestic structures. The smaller buildings in the Flagler–Era neighborhood and many other subdivisions within the city that developed at specific times in the past and spoke to the city's historical evolution were the stuff which, in the main, constituted the survey. More than 2,500 buildings in all were documented, a trove of architecture containing expressions of virtually every style employed in American building from 1821 to 1930.

At the same time, the history attached to the buildings and the neighborhoods was collected, much of the information recorded for the first time and often from sources that diminish with the passing years. The body of the survey reports thus offers a rich lode of historical ore which historians can mine for years to come. The contents of this volume represents the first published results of the survey and one of the few histories of St. Augustine that speaks about decades which in this Ancient City are often considered modern times.

William R. Adams, Director
Historic St. Augustine Preservation Board, 1977–1985

Autumn 1992
St. Augustine, Florida

A Brief Historic Overview

St. Augustine is unquestionably America's First City. It is the oldest, continuously occupied European settlement in what is now the United States. The community proudly claims its Spanish and British heritage and notes the important contributions made by a group of settlers collectively known as the Minorcans. From the first members of the ill–fated New Smyrna colony who arrived in 1777 to present members of the community, Minorcans have stabilized and enriched the city at many important points in its history. We also recognize the many important contributions made by Indians, African–Americans, and American pioneers and treat with deep respect the majestic structures that arose during the Golden Era of Henry Morrison Flagler.

Although Juan Ponce de León had sighted the coast in 1513 and named the land Pascua florida (feast of flowers at Eastertime), Pedro Menéndez de Avilés was the first European to establish and maintain a community in the area. By 1565 many European nations were intent on claiming parts of the New World. Menéndez and his fleet were pursuing French colonists led by Jean Ribault. He found the Ribault colonists at nearby Fort Caroline. In what was considered an astute military and political maneuver, Menéndez' Spanish troops massacred almost 400 men in two separate assaults. They established Spanish supremacy of the coastal area and claimed the land for Spain.

The land remained in Spanish hands for two centuries; however, the poor and unpopular settlement never produced the gold and silver sought by the early explorers. Remarkably, it was never lost in combat. The garrison town survived the attacks of Englishmen Sir Francis Drake (1586) and Robert Searles (1668). The impenetrable coquina Fort, the Castillo de San Marcos, was completed in 1695 and sheltered the community from the assault by South Carolina Governor James Moore in 1702, although he virtually destroyed the town by fire.

The noble Fort also withstood the 1740s attack by Georgia's James Oglethorpe, but the Fort could not protect the town from the political onslaught of the world powers. Spain lost Florida to England in a territorial exchange in 1763.

The British only ruled the peninsula for two decades; however, they left their mark in a few architectural reforms including adding chimneys, glass window panes, and moving entryways to the street side of the homes. Few cultural changes remained after their departure. The return of the Florida peninsula to Spain in 1783 came about when England ceded the Floridas and Minorca back to Spain in exchange for Gibraltar and other territories. But colonists of the second occupation lacked motivation. They were lethargic in their attempts to rehabilitate the former colony. The real heros of the time were the refugees from the New Smyrna colony 72 miles south of St. Augustine. Families from Greece, Italy, and the Spanish island of Minorca had been imported to Florida as indentured servants by Englishman Andrew Turnbull.

Dr. Turnbull, a medical physician from Scotland, married Maria Gracia Dura Bin of Smyrna, Greece. When Florida fell under the flag of Great Britain, Dr. Turnbull sought his fortune by acquiring land to establish an indigo plantation growing plants producing the violet-blue dye popular at the time. He enlisted a few hundred Greeks and Italians, but failing to reach the required number finally found some willing workers on the island of Minorca. The Balaeric island off Spain was a British possession at the time and had suffered from drought for several years. More than 1,000 willing workers were recruited from the island and the project was under way. The Minorcans, Greeks, and Italians arrived in New Smyrna in 1768, a year beginning almost a decade of turmoil and despair. By 1777 politics and administrative problems prompted the then remaining 600 colonists to rebel and seek shelter in St. Augustine. With the exception of the descendants of three families from the first Spanish period—the Solana, Sanchez, and Arsián–Alvarez–Gonzáles families—it was the New Smyrna settlers who remained through the British period, second Spanish period, Territorial years and Statehood. They constitute the cultural backbone of the Ancient City. The names Andreu, Capo, Genovar, Lopez, Manucy, Masters, Oliveros, Pacetti, Pomar, Rogero, and Usina are only a few of the Minorcan names which remind contemporary residents and visitors to the Ancient City of its heritage. The Greek community also has a number of families descending from the New Smyrna colonists. Names such as Genopoly, Hypolita, Llambias and Papi reflect that heritage. The recently constructed St. Photias shrine at *41 St. George Street* interprets the contributions of Greek culture to contemporary St. Augustine residents and visitors.

In 1784 politics again determined the fate of the colony and Florida was returned to Spanish rule. Houses reverted to the Spanish model with coquina a popular building material. The New Smyrna colonists became increasingly important during the period because of their economic and cultural commitment to the area. Unlike the first Spanish period, the concept of private ownership of land outside the Walled City continued, permitting many of the Minorcan settlers to become land and home owners.

When the change of flags occurred in 1821, Florida became a territory of the United States and the city underwent another metamorphosis. The government and buildings assimilated the look of the northern colonies. New pioneers settled the land. Northerners began to appreciate the climate. St. Augustine soon became known as the city of the brave and the infirm. From its earliest territorial years, Florida drew adventurous souls and those seeking a healthy climate. Ralph Waldo Emerson visited in 1827 and Prince Napoleon Archille Murat, nephew of the Emperor Napoleon Boneparte, arrived in 1824, establishing a plantation south of the city and occupying a home on the corner of *St. George and Bridge streets* which bears his name. Dr. Andrew Anderson began Markland Estate, now part of the Flagler College complex. Dr. Seth Peck maintained a residence at *143 St. George Street.* The Northerners brought their architectural styles with them and, once again, a partial metamorphosis occurred within the city's neighborhoods.

During the second Spanish period (1784-1821) the Seminole Indians had confrontations with the Americans, most notably one with Andrew Jackson in 1818. However, it is the period of 1835-1842 that marks the most significant years of battle. The Seminoles, a collection of Southern Creek Indian bands that had migrated to Florida from Georgia and Alabama in the early 18th century, had been quick to side with the Spanish against the British, and equally eager to help the British deal with the troublesome Americans.

When Florida became an American territory, the Seminoles were deeply distressed. The Americans made a futile attempt to grant them land in the central part of the state. President Jackson's Indian Removal Act of 1830 required the Seminoles to move to Oklahoma; however, they refused to budge. By 1835, small skirmishes erupted into major conflicts. After many bloody battles the Seminoles conceded and by 1842 most had been transported to Indian territory.

Exclusive of the landing of Menéndez, nothing can compare to the explosive impact of Standard Oil millionaire Henry M. Flagler. After Mr. Flagler "discovered" St. Augustine in 1884, nothing would be the same. His decision to convert St. Augustine into the playland of the wealthy changed the town forever. His magnificent hotels, the Ponce de León, Alcazar, and Cordova created a new ambiance in the sleepy Spanish town, which for the preceding several decades had tried to become "Americanized." Mr. Flagler came to St. Augustine with painful memories of his first wife's death and a need to construct a new life. St. Augustine's Golden Age reflected that desire, although it did not satisfy his needs. Mr. Flagler moved south, but St. Augustine retained his golden touch in the hotels, churches, and homes that were his inspiration.

Today, St. Augustine balances between its Ancient City heritage, its Golden Era charm, and its lust for tourist acclaim, while at the same time coping with 20th century concerns of ecology, education, industry, and growth.

No matter which aspect of the town is the focus of attention, America's First City is worthy of notice by all those who wish to understand one of the most important, but most often overlooked, landmark cities in the United States.

It is the intention of the book to provide information about architecturally and historically significant sites and structures not necessarily familiar to the general public. Buildings exemplifying specific architectural styles or periods will also be addressed. Information about many of St. Augustine's other fine buildings , not emphasized herein, is available through the Historic St. Augustine Preservation Board, the Historical Society Library, and Ancient City gift shops.

Table
of
Contents

Table
of
Contents
continued

Acknowledgments

One of the most rewarding periods of my diverse career was a year spent working with the Historic St. Augustine Preservation Board twelve years ago assisting in the survey of St. Augustine's historic sites. It was exciting for all of us to research, evaluate, and write about the architecturally and historically significant sites in the Ancient City. As I worked house by house alongside my colleagues I realized the need to impart the valuable information to the public in a stimulating and informative manner. Through the cooperation of the Preservation Board and the *St. Augustine Record* an initial series of 32 articles was published. This book provides a more detailed and permanent way to share the history and architecture of the city.

Although I was the author and organizer of the series, I received a great deal of help from several experts. Dr. Michael Scardaville, historian, wrote about the colonial era. David Nolan contributed to articles about architects and lost architecture. He remained my constant source of input while rewriting and updating all the articles. Both gentlemen deserve enormous credit for their work on the project. The primary researchers involved at the time the articles were originally published included Roberta Monteith Butler, David Nolan, Paul Weaver, and coordinator, Dr. Scardaville.

Through this book, I am pleased to offer the public the results of many years of hard work by the St. Augustine Preservation Board as it interpreted and described historic gems in St. Augustine. I am particularly grateful for the leadership of Dr. William D. Adams, then Director of the Preservation Board. It is hoped that the book will be useful for those already knowledgeable about St. Augustine and for those who wish to learn more about the town and what can be done to preserve and restore cities in a country no longer young.

I would also like to thank the staff of the St. Augustine Historical Society for its continuing assistance and fine resource materials. I also cannot thank enough or praise enough my friend and assistant Mary Sears. I am particularly grateful to my special friend and proofreader, Roberta "Sherlock" Butler. Also deserving of kudos in the course of the manuscript's development are my mother Elinor Davis, and my sister Ronni Haught.

The support of my family has been critical throughout. Thank you husband John for cooking, cleaning, shopping, and all your care giving. Thank you children Kristina and Jason for your patience, understanding, and flexibility during deadline duress.

Karen Harvey
Autumn 1992

A Streetscape of Colonial Buildings

Castillo de San Marcos, San Marco Avenue
Cathedral-Basilica, 38 Cathedral Place
City Gate, Orange and St. George streets
Government House (reconstruction)
King's Bakery, 97 Marine Street
Market Place, on the Plaza
Public Library, 12 Avilés Street
St. Francis Barracks, 82 Marine Street
Trinity Episcopal Church

Avilés Street
#20, Fatio House
#32, O'Reilly House
#36, Toledo House

Bay Street
#42 Vedder House, ruin
#46 Drysdale House,
reconstruction

Bridge Street
#46, Canova House

Charlotte Street
#20, Hahn House
#101, Snow House

Marine Street
#16 Worth House,
reconstruction
#43, Sánchez House
#53, Marin House
#56, Jones House

St. Francis Street
#14, Oldest House
#20, Tovar House
#31, Llambias Street

St. George Street
#14, Genopoly House
#37, Avero House
#43, Spanish Inn
#44, Arrivas House
#52, Avero-Watkins House
#54, Paredes House
#65, Benet House
#105, Burt House
#143, Treasurer's House
#214, Lindsley House
#224, McMillan House
#250, Murat House
#279, Dummett House

Spanish Street
#42, Triay House
#62, Fornells House

Treasury Street
#57, Montgomery House

It is hoped that this streetscape will be useful when exploring St. Augustine.

Listing provided through the courtesy of the Historic St. Augustine Preservation Board.

St. Augustine's Neighborhoods

The neighborhoods represented on the accompanying map are indicative of specific developments in and around the Ancient City. Some of the neighborhoods represent definite time periods; others overlap in geography or in ambiance.

Chapter 1. Colonial City. Sea air wafting from the Bayfront is but one reminder of early Colonial development in the area surrounding the Plaza. Buildings hugging the street line and balconies casting shadows are reminders of the city's Colonial heritage. One needs only to walk the streets between the Castillo de San Marcos and St. Francis Barracks (now the National Guard Headquarters) to feel the simple pride of the settlement that never gave up.

Chapter 2. Anastasia Island. Once the location of early defenses, the island now invites those who wish to breathe clean, fresh air and venture into tempting ocean waters. The operational St. Augustine Lighthouse shines over the island inhabitants and promises seafarers a measure of security.

Chapter 3. South of King Street. The streets south of King Street encompass both Colonial and Territorial era neighborhoods and also the important African-American neighborhood of Lincolnville. Victorian period houses mix with older masonry buildings. Maria Sanchez Creek provides a beautiful setting for large estates.

Chapter 4. Abbott Tract. Pre-Civil War homes and large Victorian residences dominate the small waterside neighborhood. The charm is increased by tree-lined streets and lanes lined with smaller cottages.

Chapter 5. Model Land Tract. The opulance of St. Augustine is reflected in grandious hotels, churches, and magnificent turn-of-the-century homes built by Henry Morrison Flagler. The neighborhood is like no other to be found in America.

Chapter 6. West Augustine. Crossing US Highway One (Ponce de León Boulevard) is almost like going to another city. The land extending approximately 3/4 of a mile west of the highway with boundaries from the north on Ravenwood Street to Oyster Creek on the south provides only glimmers of the old city. One has to travel the side roads to fully appreciate the rich heritage of the community.

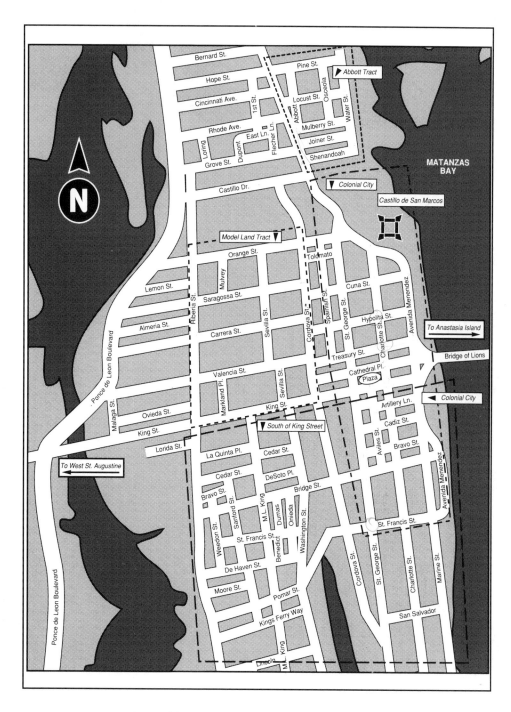

Map of St. Augustine's Historic Neighborhoods

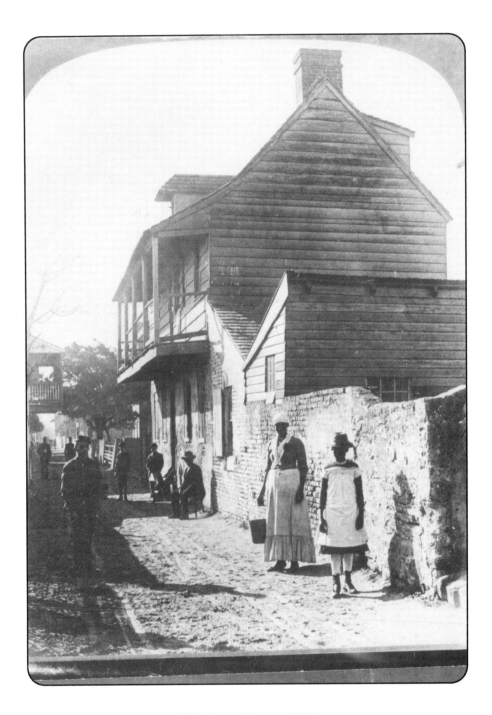

Charlotte Street, 1880

Chapter 1.
The Colonial City and Its Growth

"The aspect of St. Augustine is quaint and strange, in harmony with its romantic history. It has no pretentions to architectural richness or beauty; and yet it is impressive from its unlikeness to anything else in America.

"It is as if some little old, dead-and-alive Spanish town, with its fort and gateway and Moorish bell towers, had broken loose, floated over here, and got stranded on a sand-bank."

Harriet Beecher Stowe,
1873

Visitors to St. Augustine in the 1870s found a town unlike any other in America. The then-three-century old settlement quietly reflected its Spanish colonial charm and mystique. Within a few short years, however, the sleepy town would be shaken awake by wealthy Northerners seeking a glamorous winter retreat. Although the little "stranded" town would never be the same, it managed to retain its charm as old and new elements combined to shape the character of the 20th century city.

The community's development over the past 400 years is reflected in its architecture as well as the contributions of the people who lived and visited here. In order to understand the many facets of America's First City, it is best to begin with its colonial development, starting in 1565. Although the first Spanish settlement in Florida was in Pensacola, it was soon abandoned. St. Augustine emerged as the first, continuously occupied, Spanish settlement in what is now the United States.

First Spanish Period, 1565-1763
British Decades, 1763-1784
Second Spanish Period, 1784-1821
Territorial Era, 1821-1845
Early Statehood, 1845-1888
Flagler Golden Era, 1888-1914
Twentieth Century, 1914-present
[time periods shown in boldface are emphasized in the chapter]

On September 8, 1565, Pedro Menéndez de Avilés arrived in Florida with more than a thousand Spanish settlers and their priest. They established their first colony at an Indian village named Seloy in the vicinity of the present–day Fountain of Youth at *155 Magnolia Avenue* and the shrine called Nuestra Senora de la Leche on the Mission of Nombre de Dios grounds at *27 Ocean Avenue*. Sometime between 1565 and 1572 the growing town was relocated one mile south to the area near the present–day Plaza. The new site offered better military protection. In addition, it was on higher ground.

Menéndez and later governors laid out the community. In general, they followed existing Spanish royal laws governing the founding of new towns in Spanish America. They platted the townsite with an elongated

Map of the Colonial City

plaza near the bayfront so cargo could be easily loaded and unloaded. Property around the plaza was set aside for shops and homes for merchants. Adjacent land was also allocated for public structures such as the parish church, the governor's residence, an arsenal, and the customs house. Thus, from the beginning, the plaza became the core of the emerging community.

Narrow streets were laid out in a checkerboard pattern. The streets formed 11 small blocks: six were full–sized and five were half–sized rectangles. The resulting grid is the oldest example of a continuously occupied, urban core in the nation. Although many land use and transportation changes occurred over the following four centuries, a number of the originally platted blocks in the *Artillery Lane and Bridge street* area have retained their original size and configuration.

The government also appropriated land outside the city for essential non–military purposes. As required by 16th century *Spanish Ordinances on Town Planning in the New World*, Menéndez set aside large parcels of government–owned pasture and farmland for settlers to use to grow food for the community. By the 1580s, fields were cultivated in what is now the North City area and in the section west of town to the San Sebastian River. Privately–owned cattle were pastured on common grazing lands in North City and on government–owned corn fields after crops were harvested.

Indians and Missions

There were two Timucuan Indian villages near St. Augustine in the late 16th century. From the early days of their settlement, the Spaniards worked with the Indians to learn their ways and to establish missions near their villages. The first Christian missions established were Nombre de Dios, perhaps at the site of Seloy Village, and San Sebastian Village, on the west side of the San Sebastian River south of the present–day *King Street*. Missions were the first European attempts to convert Florida Indians to Christianity in accordance with Spanish policy in the New World. Initially, Indians from the villages worshipped with Spanish settlers in their small parish church. When Franciscan friars arrived in 1587, work began on the missions near the villages. Although a hurricane destroyed the San Sebastian mission in 1599, the Nombre de Dios mission survived into the 17th century.

In 1717 Creek Indians revolted against the English in the Carolina colony which was near Charleston, South Carolina. St. Augustine's Spanish authorities offered protection to the Creeks and, within a decade, over 1,000 Indians had resettled in 10 villages on the periphery of the Ancient City. Archaeologists have located the sites of several of the villages, including Nuestra Senora de la Leche, north of Abbott Tract; Nuestra Senora de Guadalupe de Tolomato, north of Model Land Company; Palica, along West Bridge Street in the Lincolnville area; Pocotalaca, south of South Street; and La Punta at the south end of Marine Street.

Today one can see a relocated restoration of the Mission of Nombre de Dios. La Leche, the most extensive and elaborate village contains a well–decorated coquina chapel located northwest of the intersection of *Pine and Water streets.*

Spanish Defense Lines and British Redoubts

When British troops ransacked and burned much of the then-wooden Ancient City in 1702, the Spanish crown ordered a series of earthen work defense walls built to enclose the area. Walls soon stretched across the narrow land mass north in what is today's North City. The Hornabeque, or Hornwork, was built in 1738 and extended from just below the Mission grounds southwest to the San Sebastian River. Another early defense wall was called the Cubo Line. It ran from the Castillo de San Marcos just north of present–day *Orange Street* to the San Sebastian River. The coquina pillars of today's City Gate represent an 1808 renovation of the important defense barrier. Another of the early Spanish defense walls was called the Rosario Defense Line which was roughly along present–day *Cordova Street.*

When the British captured the city, they relied on seven redoubts along the San Sebastian River to protect the western flank of the city. The western peninsula formed an essential link in the British transportation network. As witnessed by the number of times St. Augustine was captured and recaptured, the defense measures were essential throughout the Colonial period.

Mose: First American Community for Freedmen

The first African known to have arrived on Florida soil was known as Estevanico or Esteban. He was one of the survivors of the ill-fated expedition of Panfilo de Narvaez which touched the Florida coast in 1528. Earliest documentary evidence in St. Augustine dates from 1580 when 50 royal slaves were brought to the city to build and repair fortifications. By the 17th century, the Spanish crown was responsible for supplying manpower to help build St. Augustine and by the 1670s there are records of slaves arriving from Havana to work at building the Castillo de San Marcos.

Over a century before the Civil War, in October 1733, the Spanish crown declared that blacks seeking freedom in Florida, and wishing to follow the teachings of the Catholic church, would be released from bondage. It took five years for the decree to be effected and, in 1738, those who were once slaves became freedmen. Word of the Spanish decree traveled along the East Coast.

During 1738, more than 100 Africans had arrived in St. Augustine. Most had escaped slavery by fleeing from the English Carolina colony. When they reached St. Augustine and asked for refuge, Governor Manuel de Montiano arranged for the freedmen to settle in an area about two miles north of the city along the marshes of Robinson Creek, northeast of the new City Gate on the fringes of St. Augustine's northern boundary. A central village called Gracia Real de Santa Teresa de Mose was created. Governor Montiano hoped to establish small farms around the site. The village's name rapidly shortened to Mose and the area was later known as Fort Mose. The Spanish provided a priest and, when needed, soldiers to help in the community's defense. In addition to releasing all slaves living in the city, Governor Montiano attempted to bring back slaves who had been sold to families who had moved from St. Augustine to Havana.

The first small fort had a short existence. In 1740 British troops under the command of General James Oglethorpe destroyed Mose during a lengthy siege of St. Augustine. Foreseeing the danger, Governor Montiano removed all the freedmen and their families from the Mose site. The Fort was occupied by a force of British military men from the Carolina colony, led by Colonel John Palmer. The troop of 155 Britishers was effectively defeated by the Spanish militiamen and 20 of the freedmen. However, because of continuing danger, the freedmen remained in the Ancient City for almost 20 years. During the 1750s another fortification was completed at Mose and more than 60 men, women, and children felt it was safe, at last, to return to and reestablish the Mose community. A Franciscan priest served as head of the parish and the small community survived until the arrival of the British in

1763. Recent archaeological discoveries and further research on the site have been conducted by the State of Florida and the Florida State Museum of Natural History in Tallahassee has an excellent exhibit concerning the important site.

Walled City Architecture

In the 1570s, St. Augustine was described as being a "little town or village...built of wooden houses. Thatch roofs predominated, although some public structures had board roofs." By the 1600s, approximately 90% of the housing stock was built of wood or palm thatch. Although the Spanish had discovered coquina stone on Anastasia Island as early as 1580, it was only used once during the next century. In that instance, the stone was used to construct a powder magazine. Spanish Governor Mendez de Canzo had ordered coquina stone cut for a new fort after the 1599 hurricane damaged the settlement's original wooden fort. Royal officials rejected the plan to use coquina believing stone foundations would sink into the moist, sandy soil along the bayfront, and the repairs were made using wood.

For the first 300 years of its development, St. Augustine was largely a homemade city. Although royal engineers provided guidance, the outpost was largely designed by the people who lived in it. The simple dwellings were, at first, largely a product of the townspeoples' basic need for shelter. The earliest designers and builders, men knowledgeable in the fundamentals of architectural technique, were the Spanish royal engineers.

When the English founded the Carolina colony in 1670, Spaniards on both sides of the Atlantic became concerned. The Spanish crown realized the need for a fortress to protect St. Augustine, an important and strategically-located military harborfront outpost. When Spanish Governor Manuel de Cendoya was ready to begin work on the Castillo de San Marcos, he chose royal engineer, Ignacio Dazo to supervise the work. It would unquestionably become St. Augustine's most significant Colonial structure. Sr. Dazo arrived from Havana, Cuba, with a group of skilled workmen. Unfortunately, he died within seven months after overseeing the early stages of construction. Despite his death, work proceeded according to the plan he developed. In fact, when Spanish Governor Pablo de Hita Salazar attempted to change the design, he was ordered by the Crown to stick strictly to Sr. Dazo's plan. A military engineer, Ensign Don Juan de Císcaro, arrived in the early 1680s to correct errors resulting from the years of construction work done without an engineer's supervision. Other than the helpful advice of Sr. Císcara, the massive Fort, completed in 1695, was the product of Sr. Dazo's ingenuity. It is a fort that has withstood repeated and sustained cannon fire from the British and has never been conquered. Despite over 300 years of attempted invasion and weathering, it remains firmly in place guarding the Ancient City. The nearby City Gate, built around 1808 was the work of royal engineer Manuel de Hita.

After the decision to build the Fort was made, royal officials returned to St. Augustine to open the coquina quarries on Anastasia Island. By the end of the 17th century, several coquina structures were in place, including the Castillo de San Marcos, a two–story governor's residence and office west of the Plaza, and a partially–completed seawall that extended from the Fort to the foot of the Plaza. After an official reported that the quarries contained enough coquina to build four cities, the governor allowed residents to use coquina to build or add to their homes. For a short time it appeared that St. Augustine would become a coquina city. However, the invasion the Spaniards had been dreading would soon happen.

Early street scene shows Cavedo and Ximenez-Fatio houses on Avilés Street. Painted by W. *Staples Drown, ca. 1890s.*

In 1702 British Carolina Colonial troops invaded. They were led by Governor James Moore. Virtually all buildings, except the newly completed Castillo de San Marcos were destroyed during the prolonged siege and destruction of the city. Although the British were finally repulsed, the rebuilding of St. Augustine was a long, painstaking task. A hurricane in 1707 added to the disaster by destroying many of the homes that had been built during the post-siege years. As late as 1715 most residents lived in makeshift shelters constructed of straw or palm. The one exception to these crude, temporary shelters was the coquina governor's mansion. It was built between 1706 and 1713 on the site of the present–day Government House on the Plaza. Only three walls from the early 18th century building have survived.

Over the next half century, a new city gradually arose as the thatch huts gave way to small frame buildings which in turn were supplemented by structures made of coquina and tabby, a durable form of oyster shell concrete. For the first time in the city's history, most public buildings were masonry, making a strong symbolic statement to the British that the Spanish intended to stay in St. Augustine. The government built a stone guardhouse at the eastern end of the Plaza. Catholic authorities built the first coquina church and the Franciscan monastery at *82 Marine Street*, now the location of the Florida National Guard Headquarters. A residence for the bishop was built on the site that houses Trinity Parish Church at *215 Marine Street*. Stone walls for a new parish church in the southwestern corner of the Plaza, opposite the bishop's house, were completed.

Residential construction mirrored the trend. By the end of the first Spanish period, 77% of the city's 342 buildings had been constructed of either coquina or tabby. The balance of the buildings were primarily frame structures. Like their 16th and 17th century predecessors, the houses were simple, functional, and suitably adapted to the Florida frontier. Buildings generally were on the streetline and enclosed by fences or walls in order to create sufficient backyard space to plant vegetables and raise chickens. Windows rarely had glass, as the Spanish preferred board shutters to keep out the elements. Most homes did not have windows opening on the north wall where colder winter winds prevailed. Porches and loggias were placed to capture the refreshing summer breezes. Rejas, or frame window gratings, projected from the streetside to provide security and a measure of privacy. Entrances into mid–18th century homes usually were through a side yard or porch and street balconies were common. The Spanish heated their homes using braziers. Roofs were mostly pitched and covered with thatch although wood shingles were popular for public buildings.

Espinosa-Sanchez House, right foreground

Espinosa–Sanchez House

Most of the original buildings dating from the late first Spanish period have lost many of their 18th century characteristics. One particularly interesting home dating from this era is the partially restored Espinosa–Sanchez House, formerly known as the Pérez–Snow House, at 44 *Avenida Menendez*. The first documented owner, and probably the builder, was Don Diego Espinosa, part of St. Augustine's small mercantile–planter elite.

The house has undergone several major renovations and has survived two major fires. As was common in Spanish Colonial architecture, it abuts the streetline. One of the principal entrances was off the loggia to the east. Unlike most first Spanish period buildings, there was a main entrance directly onto Charlotte Street. It was added in the second Spanish period when extensive remodeling was done to convert the building from residential to commercial use. The current L–shaped configuration is similar to the original plan.

Today, only the north–south rectangular section of the building is part of the original structure. The east wing, demolished sometime around 1870 was rebuilt in the early 1920s. Four original first Spanish period arches in the loggia are the most notable features of the building. The row of round arches supports an extension of the main shingled gabled roof. The pillars supporting the arches are Neo–Classical in design with simple moldings serving as the capitals. Wood chamfered posts are found in the porch along the south end of the building. Other notable features included 9/6 windows (a Territorial design which introduced nine panes over six panes of glass), three decorative doors, and a Spanish–type chimney, built in the 1960s, attached to the east facade of the east wing. A coquina wall extends east of the north facade along Treasury Street.

Sometime between 1785 and 1798, a flat roof replaced the original wood–frame gabled roof. A second major alteration involved the addition of a coquina second floor over both wings in the late 1790s. The work was accomplished by the new owner of the property, Francisco Xavier Sanchez, the nephew of Sr. Espinosa, who used the enlarged building as a warehouse. A photograph taken around 1870 shows how the building probably looked from the late Colonial through the Civil War era. The two–and–a–half–story structure was crowned by a series of dormers sided diagonally with wood. The windows were shuttered, and there were three doors on the Charlotte Street facade, a central doorway plus two more doors at each end. The central doorway exhibited one of the best examples of Colonial post–and–lintel frontispiece ornamentation in the city. Two plain pilasters resting atop a coquina base flanked the door. The capitals were simple, similar to those on the stone pillars in the rear arcade and to others found on plans drawn by royal engineer Mariano de la Rocque in the 1790s. Moreover, three rosettes adorned the rectangular lintel which rested on the doorway and capitals.

In the 1870s, a new owner, Daniel Edgar of New York, removed the masonry second floor and probably the east wing. As in the 18th century, a flat parapet roof replaced a gabled roof. By 1884 a gabled frame board and batten second floor was built over the northern half of the structure. The addition exhibited ornamentation inspired by the Carpenter Gothic Style in vogue a decade or so before. Decorative curved lintels were placed over the four window openings on Charlotte Street and lattice was installed over the windows. The frame second floor probably was destroyed in the 1887 fire that ravaged that section of town, but the older masonry portion survived the devastation. By the mid–1890s the north doorway and the two windows flanking the central doorway had been bricked–in and plastered.

The 20th century brought another series of radical changes to the building. In the process of converting it into apartments, a shingled second floor was added over the entire masonry downstairs between 1910 and 1914. A balcony boldly projected over Charlotte Street. The south and north windows were converted into doorways and the south doorway was filled in. History repeated itself as the 1914 bayfront fire destroyed the newly–completed second floor. Once more, the up–again, down–again old building was one–story in height. Longtime proprietors of the structure, Elbridge and Fanny Snow, were responsible for the next series of alterations in the early 1920s. They built the east wing, thus returning the building to its first Spanish period configuration. In an attempt to blend the building with their new main residence along Bay Street (now Avenida Menendez), the Snows added Mediterranean Revival touches. The property was purchased by the Exchange Bank in 1963 which undertook plans to restore the house to its first Spanish period appearance. Through the years, a succession of banks have held the property while leasing it to a variety of businesses.

British Occupation

The British did not like the buildings or culture of the city they acquired and complained bitterly about the town's appearance and condition. It was too small, streets were too narrow, overall it was just "ill–built" as one Britisher of the period put it. The most direct appraisal came from a Philadelphian who wrote that "the Spaniards consulted conveniency more than taste in their buildings."

When the flags changed, there was a mass exodus of Spanish citizens. The British quickly destroyed many tabby buildings in the under–populated city and allowed empty residences to deteriorate. With little demand for housing in the first decade of British rule, the British government concentrated on refurbishing existing public buildings and putting them to different uses. The Spanish hospital became the English jail and courthouse. The La Leche Indian church just north of town became the hospital. The British put their government offices in the former bishop's house. The St. Francis monastery was adapted into barracks for the British garrison. Besides playing musical buildings, the British repaired the governor's house and the Spanish parish church of La Soledad across from the current St. Joseph's convent on St. George Street. A wooden spire was added to the existing church, and it was renamed St. Peters in 1773. British governors also made sweeping changes, particularly in the military complex in the southern part of town. Barracks were erected just beyond the newly converted St. Francis Barracks. The only remaining building dating from the British period is the coquina King's Bakery at *97 Marine Street* . It was built east of the barracks near the bayfront in order to provide fresh bread for His Majesty's troops. It now serves as offices and garages for personnel at the Military Barracks complex.

British Land Grants

Meanwhile, outside the city limits, equally sweeping changes were happening. When the British assumed control, they granted parcels of land to individuals to promote agricultural development on the underused land outside the Ancient City. Not surprisingly, British governors distributed most of what is now North City property to English subjects. The majority of the grants were under five acres, a few amounted to almost 60 acres and Anglican minister John Forbes acquired a grant that included all of what is today's West Augustine. Throughout the period, English and Minorcan settlers used the lands granted for farming and residences. The primary building material was wood with coquina, brick, and tabby.

British policy was not designed to convert Indians or to use their labor on government projects. They were segregated in a well–defined territory established west of the St. Johns River and extending into the Florida interior. Indians who journeyed to St. Augustine to receive gifts and provisions from the governor generally encamped about four miles north of town, just beyond the land grant homesteads and plantations. The British extended freedom for all blacks, including freedmen although they were restricted by a curfew, forbidden to bear arms, or leave their homes without a ticket. Even with these restrictions, the black community grew and would soon establish a neighborhood near the Walled City.

British Residential Architecture

As St. Augustine became more established in the 1770s, English property owners began to alter the old Spanish buildings. They moved entrances from courtyards to streetside and introduced glass windows, fireplaces, and dormers. Shingles replaced thatch as the primary roofing material. Despite these changes, the British retained several features of the Spanish architectural legacy, including houses built at the streetline and extensive use of balconies, porches, and loggias. Other remains of the British–built environment are found in additions, especially second stories added to first Spanish period buildings. The most notable examples are the Oldest House at *14 St. Francis Street* and the Llambias House at *31 St. Francis Street*. Both buildings are owned by the St. Augustine Historical Society, and the latter is maintained by the Altrusa Club of St. Augustine.

The Second Spanish Period

The Spanish were dismayed at the condition of the town when they reoccupied St. Augustine in 1784. They estimated that 40% of the houses were uninhabitable. The church and governor's mansion were in disrepair. Incoming Spanish Governor Vicente Manuel de Zespédes lamented that "the troops (are) without shelter, God (is) without a temple, and I (am) without a home." Many vacant residences reverted to the government. They were sold at public auction in 1790 to encourage their rehabilitation and preservation. British architectural features became an integral part of domestic and public design in the second Spanish period. Royal engineer Mariano de la Rocque mapped the city in 1788, providing an indispensable reference tool. In addition, he provided instructions for the building of the parish church, now known as the Cathedral-Basilica, which was built in the 1790s.

Spanish Defense Mechanisms and Land Grants

When they settled for the second time, Spanish governors depended less on the defense lines than had their earlier counterparts. They developed new tactics to protect the Ancient City. Contrary to long–established royal laws pertaining to the Spanish Empire in the Americas, in the 1790s the Spanish government established a liberal immigration and land grant policy. This was done as a means to convert the under–developed peninsula into an economically self–sufficient colony. Although Minorcans had unofficially occupied farm-land in North City and west of town since the late 1770s, the Spanish governors did not grant legal titles for much of that land until 20 years later. By the early 19th century, property north of present–day San Marco Avenue and in Model Land Tract, Lincolnville, and Lighthouse Park on Anastasia Island was divided into at least 50 parcels. Settlers cultivated corn and other vegetables or raised livestock in North City, while much of the land along both banks of the San Sebastian River was under citrus cultivation. The 11 grants in the Lincolnville area evolved into one elongated orange grove, from which citrus products, includ-ing orange juice, were exported to Savannah, Charleston, and New York.

Mil y Quinientas was the last major area distributed into private hands. It represented a large parcel in North City lying between the City Gate and *San Carlos Avenue*. The Mil y Quinientas, the 1,500 Spanish yard defense perimeter established shortly after 1800, repre-sented a new concept in defending the northern approach to the town. By the late 1790s, the Hornwork disintegrated and the governor was obligated to have underbrush cut in order to deprive an enemy of potential cover. Since the foliage was eliminated at royal expense, Governor Enrique White solved the problem in 1807 by bisecting the section with a new road (today's San Marco Avenue) and granted small parcels extending from the road at either side to the San Sebastian River and Hospital Creek. Conditions for receiving the grants were strin-gent. The new proprietors had to remove underbrush and trees. They could only cultivate low growing crops such as kitchen vegetables. They could not build ditches or fences. Houses had to be constructed of palm, a highly flammable material which the authorities could quickly burn if an enemy approached. The grant further stipulated that all houses had to be beside the road so that "one may be enough to set fire to all (houses) at one run." A total of 19 people, many of them Minorcans, received small grants in the Mil y Quinientas.

Sixty–nine land grants were distributed immediately outside the urban center in the late 18th and early 19th centuries. These land grants had a lasting impact on subsequent development patterns in St. Augustine. Many of today's subdivisions correspond precisely with one or multiple Spanish grants. The street plan in the late 19th and early 20th century subdivisions often paralleled the boundaries of Spanish farms, ranches, and orange groves. The northern boundary of the Mil y Quinientas, *San Marco Avenue*, remained the northern city limit until the early 1920s.

The status of the freedmen was insured during the second Spanish period. Jamaican-born Antonio Proctor arrived in Florida toward the end of the 18th century. He worked as an Indian interpreter for a British trading firm and was well established in St. Augustine when Spain and America began the War of 1812. The Spanish enlisted his aid. The multilingual interpreter later received a 185-acre grant for his services. His descendents have served in the Florida legislature and several members of the family continue to reside in St. Augustine. At about the same time that the Spanish regained control of the city, rebellion in the Caribbean French colony later known as Haiti erupted. Several black military leaders emerged. General Jose Biassou was forced to flee in the mid-1790s and found St. Augustine a sanctuary for his remaining years. Once known as Viceroy of the Conquered Territories, the black leader used his skills at Fort Mantanzas as commander of a black militia maintaining law and order south of the city. He was buried in Tolomato Cemetery in 1801.

The last 31 years of Spanish rule was a period of major home building and restoration. Many substantial coquina and frame houses remain. In addition, several public structures were erected. By 1797 the government had completed the Neo–Classical Cathedral–Basilica, at *38 Cathedral Place*. A coquina school, powder house, and blacksmith shop appeared within the following decade. Only the church has survived, although the configuration of the powder house is evident in a concrete block foundation near the St. Johns County Health Department at *180 South Marine Street*. Most remaining Colonial buildings dating from the second Spanish period are built of coquina. Genopoly House is an exception.

Genopoly House

Genopoly House is a wooden building located at *14 St. George Street*. It is the only known surviving second Spanish period frame building in the Ancient City. Built sometime after 1788, the structure shows British construction practices. This is particularly interesting since the house was built by Juan Genopoly, a Greek carpenter who was part of the important New Smyrna immigration in 1777.

Genopoly House, built after 1788

In 1776 Mr. Genopoly and two other dissatisfied New Smyrna colonists secretly traveled to St. Augustine. The men petitioned English Governor Patrick Tonyn, on behalf of the colonists, for release from their obligations. Based on the reports provided, Governor Tonyn released the New Smyrna colonists from their unhappy contract with British Dr. Andrew Turnbull. The colonists brought tremendous skill and vitality to the St. Augustine community. Their commitment to the city and their role in creating its history have been of major importance for more than 200 years.

On October 1, 1778, Mr. Genopoly purchased the St. George Street property from Jesse Fish, a land speculator during the British period. The cost was 68 pesos for the land and a building. He built a frame house on the property by 1783 and erected a second structure sometime after 1788. The second frame dwelling is the one that has survived, although with extensive alterations. Original features included a coquina fireplace and interior chimney, post and beam framing, wood liner on the interior downstairs walls in the east room, and ceiling joists and mortise joints. Other portions of the structure have been rebuilt over the centuries.

Mr. Genopoly began farming shortly after arriving in St. Augustine. In 1783 he, like other New Smyrna colonists, leased land north of the Castillo de San Marcos where he raised garden crops. In 1807 he bought land on what is now the campus of the Florida School for the Deaf and the Blind at *207 North San Marco Avenue.* At that time, the Spanish were reducing government–owned lands, and Governor White granted him a parcel north of the Mil y Quinientas defense perimeter. Mr. Genopoly gained control of his father–in–law's 25–acre tract immediately to the north and, in 1815, bought the contiguous Domingo Segui grant. On these lands he cultivated corn and other staples and developed a good sized dairy operation. In 1816 he began selling farm–grown products from his house, an accepted practice at the time.

On December 2, 1793, Mr. Genopoly, a three–time widower, married Ann Marie Barbara Simpson, a native of Baltimore, Maryland. They had four children within the next five years: Maria, George, Manuel, and John. Although Mr. Genopoly died around 1825, his property remained in family hands for many years. His North City farm and ranch were sold in 1868. The land eventually became known as the Genopoly Tract Subdivision within which the Florida School for the Deaf and the Blind and parts of Fullerwood and Nelmar Terrace Subdivisions are platted.

Genopoly House remained in the family until the death of Mr. Genopoly's grandson, John J. Darling, in 1904. Oral comments recorded in the 1930s suggest the building housed a private kindergarten shortly before the Civil War. A document dating from 1811 indicates that education fees were paid to William Lawrence, a Scotsman and tutor. It is likely that Mr. Genopoly wanted an English education for his children and perhaps himself since he had married an English–speaking woman. Also, by this time, English had become the accepted language of the St. Augustine business community. The document between Mr. Genopoly and Mr. Lawrence was written in English and an entry below the itemized fees noted that payment was given in milk, a logical arrangement since Mr. Genopoly owned the dairy.

After Juan Genopoly died in the mid–1820s, his son George became the head of the household. In 1850, the other heirs to the property, Mary Genopoly Darling and John Darling,transferred all property rights to him. By the Civil War period, the house had reverted to Mary Darling and passed to her son John after her death in 1884. Mr. Darling died in mid–1904 and bequeathed the property to his neighbors, Eunice and Frank Greatorex. Mr. Greatorex was the chief clerk of the St. Augustine Post Office at the time. The Greatorex' owned the building until 1922 and during that time leased it for commercial purposes, taking advantage of the increasing business character of north St. George Street.

Through 1918, the old Genopoly House served as the residence and novelty shop of Thomas and Cora Kearns. A 1907 photograph shows the Kearns were the first to promote the antiquity of the structure by advertising their business as being in the Oldest Frame House in St. Augustine. They also were the first to call it The Old, Old School House. In 1920, Hanna Erwin signed a five–year lease and opened a tea house in the building. Novelties and books were also sold. In 1922, the property was sold to Abraham Weinstein, proprietor of Weinstein Brothers Produce and president of the Coca–Cola Bottling Company of St. Augustine. For the next nine years, Mr. Weinstein rented the building to several aspiring businessmen who opened the Old Cedar School House Restaurant (1924–25) and the Old House Photo Shop (1927–31). Most tenants lived in the upstairs room. Mr. Weinstein sold the property to William J. Harris in 1931.

Mr. Harris, a pioneer St. Augustine photographer and long–time curator of the St. Augustine Historical Society, was the first proprietor who extensively promoted the building as a school house. He sold the Oldest School House in the United States in 1936, including the furnishings. The buyer was Clarence Lyman, then manager of the Fountain of Youth. His heirs sold it to Walter B. Fraser shortly after Mr. Lyman's death three years later. Mr. Fraser, served as mayor from 1934 to 1942 and state senator thereafter. He was St. Augustine's leading entrepreneur of historical attractions in the 1930s and 1940s. In addition to the Oldest School House, he simultaneously developed the Fountain of Youth attraction on the site of an Indian burial ground in North City. Since 1939, he has operated Genopoly House as the Oldest Wooden School House in the U.S.A. Museum.

In contemporary terms, Genopoly House experienced adaptive reuse carried to an interesting degree. The house and its owners are representative of the wide range of the city's residents who, century after century, have worked to live in, preserve, and at times, promote their Colonial era treasures.

Territorial and Statehood Structures

On July 10, 1821, the Spanish colors floated down the flagpole for the last time. Spanish rule had prevailed in the 256–year–old town for all but 21 years of British occupancy. The United States gained possession of the old town that had been laid out in the late 16th century. The configuration of the Plaza with its radiating streets remained basically unchanged during two–and–a–half centuries of growth. When newcomers viewed the city in 1821, they considered it a foreign–looking place with narrow thoroughfares and stone and frame houses built flush to the streets. Visitors were not used to seeing balconies projecting above their heads. A description written by the first American surveyor to enter America's First City called it a "ruinous, dirty, and unprepossessing" place.

There were few changes in architectural styles and elements in the early Territorial years. The settlers used coquina in the construction of walls, foundations, and chimneys. They often continued to build homes close to the streetline. Perhaps because the Minorcan population remained after 1821 and provided a sense of continuity, the change from a Spanish to an American city was done thoughtfully. Even as late as the 1840s, when statehood was imminent, Reverend R. K. Sewall described the town as wearing "a foreign aspect to the eye of the American." Although he was minister of the Presbyterian Church, Reverend Sewall had few compliments for the city. His description of

the buildings indicates most were two–story dwellings crowded together close to the streets. He noted that frequently "a piazza projected
from the base of the second story." Although he conceded the benefi-
cial aspects of the balconies, he felt compelled to note that the piazza
"awakens a sense of peril, as one passes for the first time on horseback
through the streets."

Trinity Parish Episcopal Church

As minister of the Presbyterian Church located at *264 St. George
Street,* it is expected that Reverend Sewell knew his counterpart at
Trinity Parish Episcopal Church. In any event, he would certainly have
visited the one–story Gothic building at *215 St. George Street.* The little
chapel, begun in 1825 and completed by 1831, was similar in some
respects to other Colonial and early Territorial buildings. It was
constructed with coquina and measured 36' x 50' with the northside
entrance flush to the street. Existing portions of the original church
include the north porch and cedar shingle steeple. The old coquina
walls form the north and east walls of the north transept and baptistry.
Around 1850, the chancel was expanded and a vestry room was added
to the side. Further remodeling in 1893 included the west wing and
alterations of the southeast corner. Major remodeling, however, was
accomplished in 1902. It resulted in the traditional cruciform shape of
the existing building and the repositioning of the entrance to the nave
to face St. George Street. The original St. George Street door opened
into the baptistry area in the north transept. It was at that time the first
Tiffany window was presented to the church. Renovations in 1917 and
1954 resulted in the present appearance of the church with its arched
arcade and open courtyard. The Tiffany windows have recently been
restored.

Market Place

Located on the Plaza diagonally across from Trinity Church is
another early Territorial building. The Market Place, a one–story
structure, was built in 1824 to replace a coquina building originally

constructed on the site in the early 18th century. It served as a guard-house, and parts of the structure housed a temporary market place in the early 1820s. At one time, a bell in the cupola atop the roof tolled to call villagers to the Plaza for market day. The building's use was particularly fitting as the site on the east end of the Plaza had been occupied by markets since the first one was established by Governor Canzo in 1598. Although the "new" (1824) market was severely damaged by storm and then by fire in the 19th century, townspeople rebuilt it both times. Square coquina pillars rise from the masonry floor and support a gabled roof. The structure lost its official usefulness when the public market was moved into the Flagler–built city hall in 1890.

Homes from the Territorial Era

Two of the earliest Territorial Period residences are located at *46 Spanish Street* and *33 Avilés Street*. The *46 Spanish Street* house was built between 1820 and 1833, thus making it the second oldest wooden building in St. Augustine. The frame structure was probably built by Andre Lopez after he received a land grant from the Spanish government in 1820. Traditional Colonial–Territorial elements are found in the use of coquina as piers and a hearth and in its placement close to the street. The building has been a private residence, boarding house, apartment building, and shop.

The building at *33 Avilés Street* is a two–story wooden building constructed around 1835, or earlier. The post and beam structure is framed along the lines of Genopoly House and coquina was used for the foundation and chimney. As was usual during the period, the small house was built to hug the streetline. The structure appears on the 1888 and 1893 Sanborn maps as a "tenement." By the mid–1920s, it was listed as Ben Bow Tavern and in the 1930s it became the Fireside Artcrafters and Blue Gate Gift Shop. The building was still listed as a store by the mid–1950s, but was later converted to efficiency apartments which radically altered the interior. After standing vacant for many years, it was purchased for use as a residence and long–term restoration project. All evidence of modern modifications, such as the apartment walls, have been removed and the house is slowly being returned as closely as possible to its original appearance as the owner attempts to establish a firm date of construction.

Three houses from the early 19th century have distinctive characteristics. The buildings at *76 Spanish Street, 67 Marine Street* , and *28 St. Francis Street* are one–and–a–half story frame dwellings. The *76 Spanish Street* house was built around 1840; the *67 Marine Street* home dates from between 1840 and 1854; and *28 St. Francis Street* was constructed between 1833 and 1838. It was raised above a frame first story between 1885 and 1893, giving it the current two–and–a–half story dimension. The first floor was covered with a concrete block veneer ornamented with an "x" mark on each block. All three houses have distinctive dormers displaying weather–boarding running at a 45 degree angle instead of straight across, a style popular at that time. The Marine Street and Spanish Street houses used coquina: the former possesses a coquina chimney; the latter, coquina piers. Of the three houses, only the Spanish Street house sits back from the streetline. Evidence indicates this house was moved from the lot on the corner of Spanish and Treasury streets after 1874.

Several prominent St. Augustinians were associated with the three little houses. Ramon Sabate, who built his home at *76 Spanish Street*, was city alderman in the last decade of Spanish rule. Late 19th–early 20th century owners of the *67 Marine Street* home included William S. M. Pinkham, mayor, municipal judge, and school board superintendent; and William W. Dewhurst, mayor, postmaster, and author of a book on St. Augustine history.

The house at *28 St. Francis Street* was owned by John L. Wilson and heirs between 1872 and 1923. The Wilsons were winter residents who became deeply involved with St. Augustine. Their contributions included a free library for the city and a clock placed in the Cathedral-Basilica's belfry. In 1925 the house was purchased by Maye and Charles Bagwell. Dr. Bagwell, a dentist who operated the clinic at the Florida School for the Deaf and the Blind, also had a private practice. Mrs. Bagwell remembers hearing tales of a library housed on the first floor. Her home may have served as an interim location before books were moved to the Segui-Kirby Smith building at *12 Avilés Street*. The

Bagwell family remodeled at various times with the expert assistance of carpenter and contractor Charles Leyvraz. Mr. Leyvraz, a neighbor for a time, was city commissioner in 1946. A later owner restored much of the old wood of the original house to its natural appearance.

Two houses on Bridge Street also date to the Territorial period. Number *46 Bridge Street* is a one–and–a–half story Spanish Colonial style residence constructed around 1840. The first floor is coquina covered with ashlar–scored stucco and painted pink. The house was built in 1841 by Antonio Canova for his son, John C. Canova. The frame house at *42 Bridge Street* was also built by Mr. Canova around 1840. With Greek Revival details, it originally faced St. George Street. It was built for Mr. Canova's son, Paul, who made it his home after his marriage in 1841. It was moved to Bridge Street in the late 19th century.

A firm construction date of 1839 has been assigned to the house at *59 Marine Street*. The property was owned in the late 1830s by Kingsley B. Gibbs (a member of a prominent family whose roots in the city can be traced to the arrival of George Gibbs III in 1821). In 1866 his son, Henry, operated a boarding house in the building. In 1870 the house and property were owned by Daniel Mickler, an Army captain who led a company during the Seminole War. An east wing was added in 1930 for apartments. The house possesses traditional Territorial characteristics including coquina piers and lot placement near the streetline.

The next three houses, although outside the limits of the Colonial City, are excellent examples of Territorial Period architecture. In addition, two other homes will be described in the Abbott Tract neighborhood.

Markland

Markland is located at *102 King Street*. Dr. Andrew Anderson, a physician, chose the property "outside" the city for his estate. Construction of the home began late in 1839. Unfortunately, he died shortly before the house was completed. His widow, Clarissa Fairbanks Anderson, completed the house on a slightly smaller scale than had been envisioned when her husband was alive. It was finished between 1840 and 1842. Some of the materials used were shipped from the north, including 200 casks of lime from New York. Mrs. Anderson's brother, Stephen Fairbanks, supplied numerous items including a marble hearth, knobs, hinges, pulleys, balusters, mahogany plank, and ebony furniture. Dr. Anderson's son, the second Dr. Andrew Anderson, was a prominent physician in St. Augustine and active in the community. As a friend of Henry M. Flagler, he understood the rapid growth and development which would become part of St. Augustine's gilded age. He expanded and remodeled Markland to its current Colonial Revival appearance by 1901. The grand estate is now owned by Flagler College and is on the National Register of Historic Places.

In the 1850s a two–and–a–half story Carpenter Gothic frame building was built across the street from Markland on the present site of the Post Office parking lot. The house was later moved down the street to *9 Martin Luther King Avenue*. It features extensive jigsawn ornamentation along the eaves and a classic pre–Civil War "x" pattern balustrade. It was built for Godfrey and Catherine Foster, who purchased the land in 1852 and 1854 from Mrs. Anderson. In 1859 additional property was bought from Francis Bridier. The house originally stood on six acres of land where hundreds of fruit trees were planted. Generations of the Foster family lived in St. Augustine. Andrew and Charles were carpenters and builders. Ward was a partner in Foster and Reynolds, publishers of the *Standard Guide to St. Augustine* during the Flagler era. He also operated a tourist information bureau in the Cordova Hotel. Godfrey managed a cigar factory on Marine Street that produced a hand–rolled cigar called the Foster Smoker.

Yallaha Grove and Pre–Civil War Residences

Yallaha Grove was built in the 1840s. The *115 Bridge Street* house is the oldest surviving building on St. Augustine's southwest peninsula. The one–and–a–half story residence is L-shaped with two main sections. One section is wood frame, built around 1845; the other is coquina, probably built even earlier. The entire building has a coquina wall foundation. In the 1890s, two–story shingled sections were added on the west and south sides. A later owner moved the western addition a few feet over to Weeden Street and lowered the southern addition to match the height of the rest of the building. The exterior has been restored to the basic lines as shown in two sketches of the house by E. R. Townsend that appeared in the *New York Daily Graphic* in 1876. The property had a number of different names over the years. When it was owned by a royal Spanish surgeon, it was known as Bousquet Grove. In the early American period it was acquired by Peter Mitchell, a member of the Legislative Council, and named Mitchell Grove.

When owned by Peter Sken Smith and later P. B. Dumas, it was called Yallaha Grove. Mr. Smith, a controversial St. Augustine figure, acquired the property in 1838 for $5,000 from Theodore Flotark, a St. Augustine merchant. Two years later, Mr. Smith's speculative ventures failed and he left town. His properties were foreclosed and auctioned for non–payment of taxes. Yallaha Grove was bought by Samuel L. Burrit of Jacksonville for $500 and then resold to Rose Dumas, wife of County Clerk, P. B. Dumas, who also served as Clerk of the Court in St. Johns County beginning in 1840. After his death in 1869, Mrs. Dumas and her children held Yallaha for the next 25 years. In 1893 his sisters, Stella and Rosina, sold the homestead to Michael M. Spades, a wealthy Indiana businessman.

The Spades family wintered in the Bridge Street house until 1898 when they built a house on Sevilla Street. Friends of the Spades, Mr. and Mrs. A. J. Marble, purchased Yallaha in 1899 after two winter visits to the city. Mr. Marble was a real estate man from Chicago. Because he had arthritis, an elevator was added to the west wing of the house. The property remained in the hands of the family after Mr. Marble's death in the early 1900s.

One of the Marble daughters married Jonas Coe Heartt of Troy, New York, who became involved in the St. Augustine community, serving as secretary of the Buckingham Smith Benevolent Association. Mr. Heartt died in the early 1930s and the house was left to Mrs. Frances Heartt Raub. The Raubs retired to St. Augustine and lived in the home until their deaths in the early 1950s. In 1954 the property was purchased by F. Charles Usina, a longtime member of the State House of

Representatives and co–owner of the St. Augustine Alligator Farm. William A. Forrester, a building contractor, bought the house in 1955 and did extensive remodeling. The first floor was used for several years as a welfare and food stamp office, with the residence on the second floor. Finally, Mr. Forrester and Boyd Parker built the present office on the northwestern corner of the property.

Another interesting house, located at *256 St. George Street*, is a two–and–a–half story Colonial Revival residence constructed between 1851 and 1853. A stereoscopic view in the St. Augustine Historical Society collection shows the two–story frame building with a two–story open front porch. The porch had chamfered posts and a criss–cross design in the railing, a style popular during the Territorial period. A later photograph shows the building around 1910 after it was remodeled to have a Colonial Revival appearance. The house then consisted of a one–story porch with a deck railing. A pediment with a fan light window rose between the two shuttered dormers. Round wood columns lined the porch and a small pavilion with a hip roof projected from the south side. The Sanborn Fire Insurance Maps indicated that the building was moved back on the lot between 1910 and 1917. In its current appearance the porch and pavilions have disappeared. A small portico with paired square wood columns and railings around the flat roof extends from the entrance. Shutters still accent the windows, but have disappeared from the dormers. Deed research shows a transaction in 1853 between Mauricio Sanchez, renter, and Emanuel J. DeMedicis. In 1901 the house became the property of May Barnes, a DeMedicis relative, and her husband Eugene L. Barnes. The Barnes, residents until about 1927, were associated with the real estate business.

59 Hypolita Street

The last of the pre–Civil War buildings is located at *59 Hypolita Street*. It is a two–and–one–half story residence on the streetline with two mid-19th century doors on the second floor. The exact construction date cannot be documented as one family owned the property from 1837 until 1882 and no deed transactions transpired until the 1882 date.

A house was constructed on the site between 1820 and 1833. An 1860s map shows a building on the site, but does not specify construction material. Severely altered over the years, it is now classified as St. Augustine Colonial Revival, a style developed after the 1930s that draws from real or imagined elements from the Spanish architectural heritage of the community.

Before turning to the post-Civil War period, we travel across Matanzas Bay to Anastasia Island, important from Colonial times forward.

Wooden Bridge Once Connected St. Augustine to Anastasia Island
photo ca. 1890s

St. Augustine Light during Restoration in the 1980s

Chapter 2.
Anastasia Island

First Spanish Period, 1565-1763

British Decades, 1763-1784

Second Spanish Period, 1784–1821

Territorial Era, 1821-1845

Early Statehood, 1845-1888

Flagler Golden Era, 1888-1914

Twentieth Century, 1914-present

Islands have a mystical quality, and Anastasia Island is no exception. The slender strand of white sand has been of critical importance to St. Augustine's development since the arrival of the first settlers.

In this chapter, three major trends are highlighted: The first considers the lives of the colonists as they defended their emerging city. The second recognizes the role of the island as it made the transition from watch towers to keep the land dwellers safe to lighthouses to keep those at sea safe. The third theme deals with the emerging land development patterns in the post–Civil War, Flagler, and 20th century periods.

Anastasia Island is an 18–mile–long strand of white sand. The island stretches from its northern tip to the Matanzas Inlet with the Matanzas River dividing it from the mainland. The island was named during the first Spanish period, probably for a martyred Catholic saint. The land was also called Cantera, the Spanish name for quarry, for a time. The Spanish regarded the island highly, particularly the northeast tip which provided the best site for the watch towers. Sentries manned the towers to assist ships through the narrow inlet and to warn of approaching enemy vessels.

Seaside Defenses

Sir Francis Drake was well known to the Spaniards at St. Augustine. He commanded the British fleet and was an exceptional navigator. In 1585 he led a large fleet to the Americas. His intention was to attack St. Augustine and other Spanish ports. The ships approached Anastasia Island in 1586. A sketch of the raid shows a wooden watch tower overlooking the inlet. Although it is presumed that the Spanish sentry gave warning, the warning was not enough to stop the British invaders. The wooden watch tower on the island and St. Augustine's predominantly wood and thatch buildings were in ashes when the British retreated.

As the small community of St. Augustine recovered from the raid, a second wooden watch tower was built and the Spanish crown realized the need to improve the fortification of St. Augustine. The natural deposits of coquina had just been found and determined to be of suitable strength and composition. But it was not until 1672 that work began on a coquina stone Fort. The stone blocks for the Castillo de San Marcos were slowly carved from quarries created on the island. Stones were dug, shaped, and hauled to barges waiting on the Matanzas Bay side of the island. The route from quarry to water was along a densely wooded path, now appropriately called *Old Quarry Road*. Nearby, on *Old Beach Road*, an old well and chimney south of the amphitheater mark the spot believed to have been the site of the barracks which housed the quarry overseer, Alonso Diaz Mejia, and his masons and stonecutters.

Shortly after completion of the Fort, a coquina watch tower was built to replace the wooden watch tower. That tower existed on a site approximately one-half mile northeast of the current lighthouse. Coquina was also used in the construction of Fort Matanzas at the southern end of the island. Built in 1742, Fort Matanzas protected St. Augustine from encroachment via the Matanzas River.

In 1740 British General James Oglethorpe and his troops attempted to capture the city. Today's Oglethorpe Park, deeded to the city by the St. Augustine Historical Society in 1967, is located at

Oglethorpe Boulevard and Arrendondo Avenue. A bronze marker on a coquina pillar tells the story of the 24-day period when British troops shelled the Castillo mercilessly from the site where the park is now located. The siege was unsuccessful. Cannonballs merely sank into the coquina walls of the Castillo, inflicting only minor damage. Thwarted in their attempts, General Oglethorpe's men set the still largely wooden town of St. Augustine on fire. Once again, although the Spanish had repulsed their foes, it was necessary to rebuild.

During the British Period the height of the coquina watch tower was raised and a cannon was placed on top. The cannon served as a signaling device to alert the town of approaching vessels. Barracks were built nearby and the area served as an early defense measure to protect the town of St. Augustine.

The First Light

Shortly after the United States took possession of Florida in 1821, the coquina watch tower was officially lit. In 1823–24, under the direction of the Collector of Customs, a new structure was built on the site, probably using much of the former building. By this era, although the tower remained a defense site the new light also served as a beacon for those at sea. In April 1824, Juan Antonio Andreu was appointed the first official keeper. He ignited the lard oil burning lantern for the first time. In 1856 the beacon was improved with the installation of a revolving light to replace the original 14–inch reflectors. That beacon burned until the beginning of the Civil War when Captain George Couper Gibbs, later a colonel in the Confederate Army, ordered the light extinguished as a precaution against intrusion from Union naval vessels. The light remained dark during the three years of Union occupation and did not burn again until 1867. Although the Island was primarily being used for defense of St. Augustine's residents, some settlers were moving across the Bay.

El Vergel

As you may recall, Jesse Fish sold Juan Genopoly land. Mr. Fish was a colorful, bilingual businessman and one of the island's earliest landowners. He arrived in St. Augustine in 1736 when he was about 10 years old. As an adult, he represented an English firm with offices in New York providing supplies to the little garrison town. Mr. Fish also became a planter. His forty–acre orange grove, called El Vergel, stretched across the fertile soil of the island at a point a mile or two south of the city, with the plantation house located south of the island end of the current Mickler–O'Connell Bridge on Route 312. Mr. Fish remained through the British Period and into the early years of the second Spanish era. By the time of his death in 1790, the oranges from the El Vergel grove had gained an international reputation.

Buena Vista

Another settlement on Anastasia Island in the late colonial period evolved from a 1793 Spanish land grant given to naval Captain Lorenzo Rodriquez. Captain Rodriquez cultivated the tract, approximately 124 acres of land, and named it Buena Vista. The property extended just west of the coquina watch tower to the creek bordering the coquina quarries, encompassing most of the high dunes and partially wooded areas of northern Anastasia Island. Although the land passed through many hands over the years, it remained intact until the early 1870s.

St. Augustine Light

The construction of the St. Augustine Lighthouse and Keepers' House at 81 Lighthouse Avenue that exist today was undertaken as part of a tide of redevelopment efforts following the Civil War. The decision to build a new light was made in 1869 when heavy seas threatened to topple the then-existing coquina lighthouse. Negotiations for property to build a new beacon began soon after. An offer was made by the Coast Guard to Dr. Charles W. Ballard of Albert Lea, Minnesota, to purchase five acres of land for $500, or his entire tract (now Lighthouse Park), for $2,000. Mr. Ballard was willing to sell the land once known as the Buena Vista tract, but the government moved slowly. Finally, five acres of land were purchased on May 16, 1872.

Hezekiah H. Pittee, from Maine, was named construction superintendent. It was a familiar job as he had supervised the building of many lighthouses and supply depots from Maine to Florida. A government report in 1872 comments on the "considerable difficulties and delays...experienced in procuring a valid title..." and mentions that the "stratum of compact coquina shell, called in this section of the country, coquina rock, (is) of such character as to be totally unfit to enter into the construction of a lighthouse." Apparently neither legal problems nor the selection of construction materials deterred action for long. A wharf, fuel storage building, and temporary quarters for workers were probably finished by late 1871. Brick and iron were procured from the lowest bidder and the foundation of the tower was finished by July 29, 1872. The little white building at the base of the tower still bears the date 1871, perhaps recording the completion of preliminary work. Work was suspended at least once for lack of funds. An 1873 report indicated that one benefit of the delay was the construction of the coquina jetty north of the old lighthouse to prevent further erosion. The optimistic report stated that "present appropriations should suffice" for completion of the tower.

On October 15, 1874, the new St. Augustine light brightened the night sky for the first time. The finished light was painted in a bold black and white candy–striped design. A cone roof topped the light and a black balcony with decorative cast iron brackets encircled the lower edge. The roof, balcony railing, and lower border of the light were painted red.

Back Porch of the Lighthouse Keepers' House, built 1875-1882
Image shows the 1990 restoration

The base of the lighthouse is an octagonal shape with a projecting structure. The one–story brick building, painted white, has a central hall leading into the tower. Rooms on each side of the hall once served as storage spaces for the casks of oil that powered the beacon before electricity was invented. The entrance is shielded by a gabled hood supported by eaves brackets with an attractive pendant hanging from the center. Granite was used for the stoop and as a belt course around the building. Granite window sills and decorative brick arches are two of the features of the storehouse that match elements of the large keepers' house across from it.

In 1873 $20,000 was requested for the construction of a keepers' dwelling and money was approved in that year's congressional session. By the 1875 report, the dwelling had been roofed in, the verandas built, and the floors laid. By 1876, the building was completed and enclosed by a brick wall. Early photographs show that the wall had a geometric pattern of open spaces and bricks, somewhat resembling lattice work. The keepers' house was designed as a two–story duplex with interesting architectural details. The eaves were decorated with thick–carved brackets. The two–story porches on the east and west sides had chamfered posts and jigsawn brackets. Metal stars at the ends of the reinforcement rods decorated the exterior walls between the first and second floors. The chimneys had corbelled brick caps. Granite sills and door jamb, and decorative brick arches added to the beauty of the building. Although the walls were brick, the foundation was made of cut blocks of coquina. Arched doorways on each side of the central hallway opened into separate apartments. Longtime residents of Lighthouse Park recall that the keeper lived on the north side of the building, the assistant on the south side. A request was made in 1882 for $2,500 to build two kitchen wings and remove the old frame structures which were "unsightly." An early photo taken from the top of the lighthouse shows a formal garden on the west side of the house. A 1914 surveyor's report listed the foliage as "dense live oak, magnolia, cedar, holly, and palmetto scrub."

From the day of its completion, the lighthouse attracted tourists. Before the wooden bridge across the Matanzas River was completed in 1895, the South Beach Ferry Company transported visitors to the island every hour, commencing at 9 am. The trip across included a five–mile train ride to South Beach and stops at all "points of interest." An advertisement in 1893 indicated the lighthouse could be climbed by interested parties: "The view from the top of the lighthouse is one of the finest in the country. To visit this, the beautiful beach of Anastasia Island and the coquina quarries, take the ferry at the foot of the Plaza."

W. A. Harn was one of the earliest lighthouse keepers. He held the position in the 1880s. His daughter, Ruby, was present on June 20, 1880, when the old coquina tower finally crashed into the sea. The keeper's log for that date states that "the old tower fell at 5 P.M. Very high tide." Mr. and Mrs. Harn and their daughters were gracious hosts to many visitors who wanted to tour the lighthouse while on the island. After Mr. Harn's death, his widow continued the work until the mid–1890s when the family moved to Enfield, Maine.

For most of the first quarter of the 20th century, Captain Peter Rasmussan was in charge of the beacon. During his tenure, coquina concrete posts marking the boundaries were built in 1914 under the direction of U.S. Surveyor Murray E. Gilderbloom. In 1924, Captain John Lindquist replaced Captain Rasmussan as keeper.

On March 2, 1936, the lighthouse was electrified, a process which completed the progression from the lard oil lamp of 1874. The keeper at the time was Chief C. D. Daniel, who had served as assistant in 1910. Mr. Daniel's first assistant at the time the light was electrified was David Swain who later served as caretaker of the light from 1956 to 1968. The Fresnel lens was a rotating glass enclosure of alternating prisms providing a pulsating flash every 30 seconds. It could be seen 19 miles out at sea. By 1939, the U.S. Coast Guard took over the U.S. Lighthouse Service and dimmed the light from 20,000 to 5,000 candle-power as a wartime precaution.

The last keeper of the St. Augustine Lighthouse was Coast Guard Chief James L. Pippin, who retired in July 1955 at the age of 68 after 28–1/2 years of caring for lighthouses. When Chief Pippin retired, control of the light was switched to automatic. After that change, a lamplighter who lived elsewhere served as caretaker for the light. In addition to Mr. Swain, Henry R. Mears held that position.

In 1969 the property around the lighthouse was declared surplus by the U.S. Government. The area included the keepers' house which was reported in rundown condition. The City of St. Augustine expressed interest in acquiring the property; however, the purchase did not materialize due to lack of funds. On July 20, 1970, the St. Johns County Board of Commissioners voted to purchase the house. Eight days after the county's decision, an early morning fire, believed to have been an act of vandalism, gutted the dwelling. Regardless of the damage, the county purchased the property on April 15, 1971, for $29,000.

For 10 years the blackened timbers of the skeletal remains of the keepers' house stood silently as the community debated over the building's fate. Although the interior was heavily damaged, interior details were still discernible including beaded–edge wooden wainscoting and coquina hearths accenting most of the eight fireplaces. Several efforts to save the structure failed. In 1981 the tower and keepers' house were given National Register status thus paving the way for restoration by the Junior Service League of St. Augustine which adopted the project in 1980. In 1982 the league signed a 99–year lease with St. Johns County and embarked on a lengthy restoration project which cost about $500,000. In 1988 the beautifully restored building was opened as the Lighthouse Museum. In addition to maritime exhibits and lighthouse–related displays, the building contains a gift shop and a fully operational kitchen. The second floor was converted into a one–room gallery and meeting room. The museum and gallery are operated under the sole direction of the League.

In April 1990 the Junior Service League signed a lease with the Coast Guard enabling them to open the tower to the public and restoration work began. Unfortunately a major setback occurred in 1991. It was discovered that damage incurred in 1986 when vandals shattered several of the lens prisms with high powered rifle shots had created problems far worse than broken glass. Although the light remained functional, the rotation of the glass cage caused damage to the prisms, forcing the Coast Guard to turn off the light in September 1991. A temporary light with a less effective beam was installed.

Replacing the Fresnel lens was a tremendous problem. Prisms of that type are no longer produced and reproduction would be a time consuming and expensive process. Fortunately, a breakthrough occurred early in 1992 when an innovative process was discovered by which medical technology was used to help save the lens. A 3–D industrial digitizer, usually used to diagnose skeletal abnormalities, was used to scan the lens and provide accurate measurement details. FARU Technology of Orlando, Florida, donated its expertise to duplicate the damaged prisms. The work is in process and St. Augustinians and sailors eagerly await the full return of "their" beacon.

Lighthouse Park

Soon after the U.S. Government bought the five–acre parcel of the old Buena Vista property as the site of the new lighthouse and keepers' house, the balance of the old Rodriquez tract was sold to James Renwick in 1872.

Besides its beautiful architecture, Mr. Renwick probably selected St. Augustine because his wife Anna had family ties in the city. By the time they settled in St. Augustine, Mr. Renwick was already well known as a brilliant architect and pioneer in the introduction of Romanesque and Second Empire styles in the United States. He is remembered internationally for his designs of the Smithsonian Institution and the William W. Corcoran home (now the Renwick Gallery) in Washington, D.C. The Corcoran home, completed shortly before the Civil War, was one of the first major examples of Second Empire design in America. Fortunately for St. Augustine, Mr. Renwick was also experienced in church architecture, having designed St. Patrick's Cathedral in New York. In 1887 a disastrous downtown fire gutted the Cathedral of St. Augustine (now known as the Cathedral-Basilica). Town leaders approached their island neighbor. Mr. Renwick served as the architect for the Cathedral's reconstruction. He added the bell tower, designed the bishop's throne, pulpit, and altar of the Blessed Virgin to the left of the main altar. The bell tower, his most distinctive exterior feature, was constructed of poured concrete, a newly discovered process used in many St. Augustine buildings of the period. In the

1960s, the exterior of the Cathedral-Basilica was covered with stucco as part of its much needed renovation.

Sometime between 1879 and 1886 the Renwicks sold their property to the William Aspinwall family. An 1879 sale shows five acres of property purchased by W.S.M. Pinkham. Mr. Pinkham, a businessman, hotel proprietor, and once mayor of St. Augustine, sold the island property to Paul Capo in 1882. The tract became a subdivision which now bears his name. It is bordered on the north by Carter Street and extends south along the west side of the lighthouse property. Mr. Capo's appreciation of ocean property later led to the development of Capo's Beach on land north of the inlet. Between 1885 and 1886 Moses Bean bought 50 acres of the remaining Aspinwall land. Mr. Bean, a New Englander, was a partner of St. Augustine residents Dr. Charles Carver and Colonel Milo S. Cartter. The Bean–Carver–Cartter partnership quickly developed several subdivisions on the land, one being known as Lighthouse Park.

The origin of the street names in Lighthouse Park is generally easy to determine: Lighthouse Avenue, Ponce de León, Palmetto, Magnolia, and Ocean Way are a few of the obvious names. Carver Street is named for one of the developers; White is for Utley J. White, and Busam was for one of the early entrepreneurs. The three partners went to great lengths to promote Lighthouse Park. The Octagon House lot at 62 Lighthouse Avenue was one of the first two purchases made in what area residents called "The New City of Anastasia." Henry Flagler was another early land purchaser in the area whose lot on the corner of Lighthouse Avenue and Carver Street still remains vacant. Many of the early investors in the Lighthouse Park area were northern friends of the developers. Their dreams of financial success never materialized as early high prices plunged by 90% within the first decade.

Lighthouse Avenue

The northern tip of Lighthouse Avenue was popular in the Victorian era. Three houses date from between 1886 and 1899 and two "later" homes were built between 1900 and 1910. The lots comprising the property at *5 Lighthouse Avenue* and a portion of the site of *7 Lighthouse Avenue* have closely related early histories. Through a series of real estate transactions, portions of the land passed from the developers, Mr. Carver and Mr. Erwin, to Albert Lewis and W. W. Dewhurst. The land was then sold to Oscar B. Smith and James E. Ingraham. Mr. Lewis was a wealthy lumberman from Bear Creek, Pennsylvania; Mr. Dewhurst was the successful proprietor of the St. Johns County Abstract Company; Mr. Smith served as a state senator in the 1890s; and Mr. Ingraham was Mr. Flagler's chief lieutenant in the development of St. Augustine.

By 1887, the property at *5 Lighthouse Avenue* was owned by Senator Oscar B. Smith, also president of W. Lyon Company, a large retail outlet. He built a one–story frame dwelling between 1895 and 1899. He sold the cottage in 1914 to Robert L. Gibson, an inventor and designer of parts used by the Victor Talking Machine Company. Mr. Gibson made the cottage his winter residence until his death in 1918. His widow Anna held the house until 1945 when it was sold to Elizabeth and Carl Turschwell, antique dealers. For a time in the 1950s, the house was owned by Thomas M. Carnegie, Jr., a nephew of Andrew Carnegie, the steel baron. In 1955 it became the property of Ernest L. and Elizabeth Little who lived in the home until Mr. Little's death in 1979. Mrs. Little died a few years later leaving the home to her son and grandson who still maintain ownership. The house has been enlarged and remodeled over the years concealing its original Victorian appearance.

Mr. Ingraham built a one–story frame vernacular dwelling at *7 Lighthouse Avenue* between 1907 and 1910. It was the family's beach cottage until 1943. At various times, Mr. Ingraham served as vice president of the Florida East Coast Railway, president of the Model Land Company, and mayor from 1915–1920. His primary St. Augustine residence was at *32 Sevilla Street*. In 1943 the Ingrahams sold the property to Charles E. Shepperd, president of the Record Press, Inc. Boleslaw and Laura Kontoft owned the house in the 1960s and in 1968 it became the home of Ann and Jesus (Rico) Belmonte.

A cottage at *8 Lighthouse Avenue* was the home of Moses R. Bean. It was built in 1886 and was often mentioned in the county newspaper which predicted a great future for the new city of Anastasia. Mr. and Mrs. Bean and their daughter, Florence, were active in St. Augustine society and entertained frequently. He also owned and rented other cottages on the island. Mr. Bean died in 1896. In 1899 his widow and daughter left the ocean–side cottage. For the next four years the house was owned by Lauriston S. Smith, a senior partner in the Smith and Woodman Drug Store. From 1904–1906 it was owned by W. H. Erwin, one of the pioneer growers in Hastings, Florida. The house then became the property of Winifred Erwin Littlefield and her husband, Chester. Mrs. Littlefield was Mr. Erwin's daughter and the niece of Utley J. and Sarah White, another prominent St. Augustine family of the period. Mr. Littlefield was a second assistant wireless station operator at the U.S. Naval Wireless Station a few yards away. A later occupant was Alice Lawton who had been art editor of the *Boston Post* for almost 25 years before retiring to St. Augustine. Although the cottage has been altered and remodeled over the years, it still retains the pierced and jigsawn work in the gable reflecting its Victorian origin.

One of the more distinctive homes in the area is located at *10 Lighthouse Avenue*. The house, built between 1887 and 1894, began as a small, one–story cottage. It was originally built for Mrs. Mary Eliza Shands of St. Louis, Missouri. She sold it in 1897 to Miss M. A. Sharman of Thomaston, Georgia, and in 1905 it was purchased by Mr. Erwin. By 1917 two open porches were added. Shortly after 1920 Mr. Littlefield formed a potato farming partnership with the Erwins in Tocoi, Florida, near Hastings. The Littlefield family moved from *8 Lighthouse Avenue* to *10 Lighthouse Avenue*. By 1924, four years after the Littlefield's acquired it, the cottage was raised to become a two–story home. Six years later it was again considerably expanded on the north side. A three–story tower was added which provided a uniquely Victorian look. A clay tile cornice, ornamental spindlework, and ceramic tiles on the first–floor porch added a Spanish touch. A surrounding wall adds an interesting effect with concrete blocks of varying patterns. The Littlefields sold the property to James G. Hempstead in 1925. In 1942 it was purchased by Jack Acebal, operator of a vending machine company and package store, and has been in the Acebal family ever since.

Rollin N. Clapp bought the lot at 62 *Lighthouse Avenue* for $350 in 1886. He built the Octagon House, one of the most interesting residences in the area. It is the only classic Octagon–style house in St. Augustine, a late example of the national trend which started in the 1850s. Mr. Clapp was familiar with the work of Orson Squire Fowler, an amateur architect, who had published *A Home for All, or The Gravel Wall and Octagon Mode of Building.* Mr.

Fowler claimed the octagonal design enclosed 20% more floor space than a square with the same length of wall, was more beautiful, and more in harmony with nature. Mr. Clapp agreed. In addition to its shape, other architectural features of the house include a Chinese Chippendale balustrade around the open second–story porch and on the widow's walk. Jigsawn porch and cornice brackets decorate the exterior. Two wings on the west and north sides were later additions.

Contemporary View of Octagon House

Without adequate transportation to and from the island, St. Augustinians of the late 19th century were not ready to move to the beach. When Mr. Clapp sold the Octagon House and property in 1905 he realized only $625 for both—$275 more than he had spent for the land almost two decades earlier. Bettina Kuhn bought the house. Her husband, R. E. Kuhn, was a furniture dealer. A few months after buying Octagon House, Mrs. Kuhn also bought two adjoining lots from Colonel Milo Cartter's widow, Isabella Cartter. Those lots, for which she paid $165, later became the property of Sarah White. The Whites incorporated the Octagon House into their family compound. Mr. White died in 1917, In 1923, Mrs. White sold several Anastasia

Island properties to H. W. Davis, including the Octagon House. Mr. Davis rapidly acquired land along both sides of Lighthouse Avenue, between White Street and Busam Street. He was a St. Augustine merchant and board member of the First National Bank of St. Augustine and the People's Bank for Savings. Mr. Davis lived in the Octagon House for more than 20 years.

In 1945 Norman MacLeish, an artist from Glencoe, Illinois, bought the property, a 50–foot lot on the east side of Lighthouse Avenue, and the old U.S. Navy Wireless Station on Carver Street. His brother was Archibald MacLeish, Pulitzer Prize–winning poet and dramatist. After about 10 years, Mr. MacLeish sold the Octagon House to Thomas and Eugenie Shackford of Illinois and in 1962 the heirs of the Shackford estate sold the home to Mrs. Marion T. Warren, a clerk in the County Tax Assessor's office. After 1965 a St. Augustine architect renovated and restored the interesting and unique structure.

White Mansion

Although Utley and Sarah White did not build the pioneer home in Lighthouse Park, it is evident from site histories that their house would have great influence on the development of the area. The Whites purchased several lots to create a family compound with a waterfront view. The White Mansion was built at *60 Lighthouse Avenue* in 1912. The marble front steps were included to honor a promise he had made his wife. The two–and–a–half story masonry residence was built of brick with a shell dash stucco finish. The concrete block wall that surrounds the compound forms an important part of Lighthouse Park's appearance. After Mr. White's death, Mrs. White continued to occupy the mansion until 1923 when she sold it to Mr. Davis.

In 1953, after Mr. Davis' death, his daughter Wilma transferred ownership of the property to the trustees of the Preachers' Relief Fund of the Florida Conference of the Methodist Church. This was a natural arrangement since she had devoted her life to the church. Dr. Wilma Davis grew up as a member of Grace Methodist Church in St. Augustine where her father served as Sunday School superintendent for 50 years. She received her bachelor's and master's degrees in education from Stetson University, graduating in 1919. In 1959 she received her Ph.D. from Boston University. From then until the 1970s she worked for the church performing ministerial services for numerous Florida congregations and traveling extensively. The much admired former minister is over 100 years old. Her former home, the White Mansion, is now an apartment complex.

Victorian Residences

An interesting house at 74 *Lighthouse Avenue* presents a bit of a puzzle. Although the house appears to belong as a Lighthouse Park early period building—those constructed in the 1880s and 1890s—the lot on which it stands was vacant in December 1912 when Sarah White purchased the property for $250. The 1894 bird's–eye sketch did not include the site. Instead, the Lighthouse and the Octagon House were shown side–by–side, an unlikely circumstance, but one with no explanation.

An early photograph of two fishermen shows an old house in the background. The unique paneling around the doorway provides unmistakable identification, although the house in the photograph is set on a brick pier foundation. The mystery is solved when it is realized that the house at 74 *Lighthouse Avenue* was moved from the lot now occupied by the White Mansion. It must have been a quick trip down the avenue for the two-story frame building, built sometime between 1886 and 1894, since it was comfortably in place on concrete blocks on its southern lot at Number 74 by the

Fritchieff Monson on left, person on right not identified, photo ca. 1880

summer of 1912. Although the original wood siding has been covered with asbestos shingles, Victorian elements including novelty shingles, spindle balustrades, and turned posts on the balcony remain intact. It was sold to J. T. Speights, a farmer from Elkton, Florida, and remains in his family.

Ponce de León Avenue

Ponce de León Avenue on Anastasia Island can be confused with the highway in St. Augustine in name only. The island version is a little thoroughfare. It was not even cut through when the older houses that face it were built.

The house at *5 Ponce de León Avenue* is situated on one of the highest locations in the city, affording occupants a view of the water from the upper stories. The two–story building was constructed in 1910 and received its three–story tower sometime after 1930. It was built for William J. Russell, the chief electrician at the U.S. Wireless Station. After being transferred in 1917, he sold the property to Felix Fire who sold it to George Reddington. Mr. Reddington lived in the home for many years. In 1941 Mrs. Reddington sold the house to W. I. Drysdale. It changed hands again in 1944 when Slade D. Pinkham and his family purchased the home. Mr. Pinkham was one of the longtime directors of the St. Augustine Historical Society.

A most unusual house stands at *15 Ponce de León Avenue*. The three–and–a–half–story Victorian frame residence consists of a masonry first floor, a wooden second–story with novelty siding, and a wood board and batten third level. The board–and–batten siding, distinguished by the vertical placement of boards of two different widths, is a very early construction method of which few examples remain. An explanation for the construction and an accurate description of the evolution of the house is difficult to determine, particularly due to confusion caused by the 1894 birds–eye sketch. No house appears on the site at the time of the map; however, financial transactions in 1890 and 1898 indicate a house may have been present. The original property owner, Orange Howes, operated a skating rink on

Maria Sanchez Creek. He mortgaged that property in 1890, possibly to construct a residence. Mr. Howes, also a postmaster on the island, sold the property in 1895 for a price which indicates there was a home on the land. The property was bought by Florence and Clarence Bevan who were reported in a local newspaper as residing in their beach cottage in 1899. When the property again changed hands, furniture was mentioned in the transaction. Eventually acquired by J. D. Rahner, the lot containing the house and two others was purchased by the White family in 1913. It appears that house moving was no problem during the period as the house may well be the combination of at least two houses, both stacked on top of a masonry first floor constructed during the period between 1910 and 1925.

Castle Betsworth

The "castle," as Captain William Betsworth called it, is situated on a sand dune covered coquina ledge at the corner of Ponce de León Avenue and White Street at 46 White Street. It is one of the oldest houses on the island and one of the most distinctive. The intersecting gable roof rises in the salt air, announcing the presence of the two–and–a–half story structure. Decorative work in the clipped gables accent the unusual roof. Captain Betsworth purchased the property in 1886. The house is of frame construction on a masonry first floor which was considered a raised basement, one of three of that type along Ponce de León Avenue. The wrap–around porch has decorative chamfered posts and jigsawn brackets and balustrades. Captain Betsworth came from Baltimore, Maryland. He kept the American flag floating in the island breezes from a standard on his property. Society news items note that he had numerous international guests.

Captain Betsworth died in the 1890s leaving his widow Addie to sell the property. She apparently held a less pretentious view of the "castle," as she referred to it as Oriole Cottage. An attempt in 1899 to sell the cottage failed. In 1901 the home was rented by Mr. and Mrs. Thomas Jackson who again adapted the "castle" designation. In 1904 Realtor Eugene L. Barnes bought the house and resold it shortly thereafter. From 1910 to 1913 it was owned by Marion Hamphill

Royston, the postmistress on Anastasia Island. Her late husband, Herbert A. Royston, had been engineer of the South Beach Railway, a small steam locomotive that carried passengers two miles south on the island to the Alligator Farm. In 1913 Mrs. White added Betsworth Castle to the family's properties. In 1920 she sold the property to Felix Fire. Numerous families have lived at Castle Betsworth since Mr. Fire's occupancy. For a time the castle was converted to apartments and then restored to a single–family house. The wrap–around porch is now partially enclosed, although the original chamfered posts and jigsawn work remain intact.

Also in Lighthouse Park

Shepharin Busam and his wife Mary arrived on Anastasia Island around 1908. Initially, they delivered mail and performed other services in the community. They established a filling station and store in the five-sided building at *37 White Street*. The building is now a private residence and serves as an interesting example of a recycled building.

Directly across from the Busam's store is the masonry building at *37 Magnolia Drive*, once the Cozy Inn. By 1924, Mrs. Mary H. Heston was proprietor of the inn and served as the island's postmistress. One of the guests who came for several winter seasons was Arthur Brisbane, a New York journalist. The Inn is now a private residence.

Built between 1910 and 1917, the home at *35 Magnolia Drive* is one of the earliest dwellings made with locally produced coquina block. The front steps and facade feature extensive ornamental ceramic tile work and the basement is one of the few built in St. Augustine.

Although the focus has been on Lighthouse Park, several other areas on Anastasia Island were also of primary importance during the area's development. One of the earliest residences outside the Lighthouse Park subdivision is located at *434 Carver Street*. The two–story, frame, octagonal residence was built in 1905. The building was used as a U.S. Navy Wireless Station and served as a government telegraph station from 1905 until after World War II, although it had been reduced to part–time status as early as 1925. The property was bought by Thomas W. Keegan after the war and is now a private residence.

Old Quarry Road

Alaise was the name given to the large Hecksher estate located midway down the road at *400 Old Quarry Road*. The house is behind a gate with massive stone pillars. The winter home was a two–story, wooden, shingle residence built around 1925. It included significant details such as a clay tile roof and a corner window with decorative bungalow brackets adding to its appearance. August Hecksher was a New York millionaire who served as a director of a number of major U.S. corporations including Crucible Steel Company of America, the Empire Trust Company, and the Equitable Office Building Corporation. He also invested in Florida real estate and owned and developed Vilano Beach on the north side of St. Augustine Inlet in the 1920s. He built the palatial Vilano Beach Casino on North Beach. It opened in 1927, but was undermined by the sea within a few years.

During the early 20th century ferry, rail, and automobile transportation made living on Anastasia Island practical. The A. B. Day House at *404 Old Quarry Road* was built between 1910 and 1917 and was one of the earliest homes in the area. Gould T. Butler, a St. Augustine architect, incorporated wood shingle siding, palmetto tree porch posts, and a foundation of coquina concrete block. The building was used as a kindergarten for a time. The scenic beauty of the area was not lost on filmmaker Peter Bogdanovich who partially filmed *Illegally Yours* at the house in 1988.

Davis Shores

The extreme northern tip of Anastasia Island is far different today from the marshlands the Spanish found. None of St. Augustine's conquerors inhabited the area for almost four centuries. In 1855, the Federal government promoted the development of public lands under the mantle of the Internal Improvement Fund and granted land to several public transportation firms. From 1858 until 1907 the bulk of the land now known as Davis Shores was owned by the St. Johns Railway Company, the Florida East Coast Railway Company, and the St. Augustine and South Beach Railway and Bridge Company. Two officers of the latter company, H. J. Ritchie and M. R. Bean, were instrumental in establishing a trolley across the marshlands to the shores of the new city, Anastasia.

In 1925, D. P. Davis, a Tampa land developer, arrived. He had successfully filled in a lowlying land area and created a residential island area near Tampa, Florida. Using similar landfill techniques, he reshaped the tip of Anastasia Island and began building Davis Shores. One of the original structures is a two–story Mediterranean Revival residence at *10 Montrano Avenue*. The house has such traditional features as textured stucco and a red clay–tile roof. What is now the Knights of Columbus Hall at *121 Arredondo Avenue* was built around 1925 as the administration building for the Davis Shores properties. Another of the original Mediterranean Revival Style homes is located at *307 Minorca Avenue*. It became the home of Harold Ryman of Ryman–Thompson Real Estate, the firm that originally marketed the Davis Shores properties. Unfortunately Mr. Davis' dream for the land was unfulfilled when he disappeared at sea in 1926.

Anastasia Island is no longer the pristine barrier island it was during the Spanish, British, and Victorian eras. Contemporary condominiums line the coast along the southern end and state recreational parks provide easy access to beaches and inland waterways. Little has changed, however, in the beautiful lighthouse area where the Lighthouse Park neighborhood retains its eclectic charm.

We now leave the history, people, beaches, and buildings that are part of Anastasia Island's heritage and return to St. Augustine's Colonial era.

On the dunes, Anastasia Island, ca. 1914

Palm Row, houses built early 1900

Chapter 3.
South of King Street

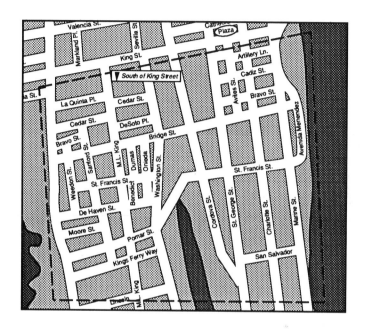

First Spanish Period, 1565-1763

British Decades, 1763-1784
Second Spanish Period, 1784–1821

Territorial Era, 1821-1845

Early Statehood, 1845-1888

Flagler's Golden Era, 1888-1914

Twentieth Century, 1914-present

The area south of King Street combines Colonial, Territorial, and Victorian architecture. Although the emphasis is on residential development, there are also a number of extraordinary public buildings to be seen. When walking these tree-lined streets, it is important to realize the area was the first to be permanently settled.

Early History

An archaeological event of great importance occurred in what is now *One Palm Row's* front yard. Historians had known of the Spaniards' early settlement of the area for a long time. In 1978 a search finally began for the home of Francisco Ponce de León, a high military official during the first Spanish period who was known to have lived in the area. During the dig one of the oldest wells in St. Augustine was discovered. Although the location of the house was not confirmed, the well, when evacuated, produced pottery fragments dating back to the late 1500s. It is one of the oldest wells showing European occupancy of North America. The team of archaeologists, led by Dr. Kathleen Deagan of Florida State University, dug on property fronting both *One and Two Palm Row*. A 1588 map shows a house located somewhere in the vicinity. Later maps of the first Spanish period also show a building or buildings on the site.

In 1991 a second well was discovered by a team of archaeologists. Dr. Deagan, then with the University of Florida, led the first effort. Dr. Stanley Bond of the Historic St. Augustine Preservation Board led the second dig. The round coquina well, located opposite the O'Reilly House at *32 Avilés Street*, dates from 1613. It was one of the first examples of the use of coquina by early settlers. When uncovered, charred furniture parts, cooking utensils, and other household items were found. It is believed that they were the remains of the vicious attack and burning of the city by pirate Robert Searles in 1668. These two wells provide an outstanding sense of the continuity of settlement in the area. We now turn to residential architecture.

In 1832, Dr. William Simmons purchased the property from the de Castro family. Dr. Simmons was a St. Augustine physician and author of a book describing the Seminole Indians and his travels through Florida during the winter of 1822. He sold the property to Hannah Douglas, wife of Thomas Douglas, then District Attorney for East Florida and later a Florida Supreme Court Justice. When Mrs. Douglas bought the land, it was covered with fruit-bearing trees. Although Judge Douglas died in 1855, Mrs. Douglas retained the property until 1873 when she sold it to John P. Howard, a wealthy New Yorker. The property was transferred to Amos Spear of Vermont and finally purchased in 1886 by Dr. E. M. Alba, a physician and pioneer druggist who served as mayor in 1883–1884. At the beginning of the 20th century, Theodore Parson Hall of Detroit, one of St. Augustine's winter residents, bought the land. His plans for its development did not materialize and it was he who sold the parcel to Henry Philip Ammidown in 1904.

Mr. Ammidown's interest in the Ancient City probably developed from his father's earlier involvement with St. Augustine. Henry's father, Holmes, had been a prominent Boston and New York merchant who built and occupied a large residence on the site now occupied by the Webb Parking Lot on St. George Street. The senior Mr. Ammidown had served in the Massachusetts Legislature in the 1830s and helped establish the Board of Education in that state. In St. Augustine he promoted public education and beautified the Plaza area by planting orange trees.

Palm Row

In March 1904, the *St. Augustine Evening Record* informed residents that a large empty lot east of the Alcazar Hotel, was soon to be developed. Houses would be equipped with all modern conveniences, including baths and hot and cold running water. The *Evening Record* praised the plan of constructing artistic and ornamental dwellings and expressed delight at the prospect of having a thoroughfare cut through from Cordova to St. George Street. The new street, to be named Palm Row, would be paved with brick. It was emphasized that stately palms would be planted to enhance the thoroughfare. A great deal of community excitement surrounded the development of the Palm Row homes. The original plan included 12 houses, only six were completed.

Emotion heightened in 1905 when workmen planting a palmetto tree found six dollars in old Spanish and Mexican coins, the largest coin being a silver dollar. Although the dates of the coins were not noted in the reference materials, from today's vantage point, the finding of the coins may have been a "sneak preview" of the important discovery of the early wells.

Now, almost 90 years after being planted, many of the original palmetto trees still stand. A brick road runs in front of the late–Victorian style homes. The houses share common architectural details such as gable roofs, gable hoods over the doors, shuttered windows, corbelled brick chimneys, and brick pier foundations. Jigsawn brackets, bargeboards, and chamfered wood posts emphasize the Victorian design. Etched glass in the doors and balconies on the attic level contribute to the unique style. Although some architectural features have been lost over the years, many remain. Novelty wood siding, a distinctive building material popular from the 1880s to the 1920s, has remained intact on all but one of the houses. Five dwellings line the south side of the brick thoroughfare: they are numbers *One and Two Palm Row*; a duplex numbered *Three-Four Palm Row* (which originally used only the number 3); and numbers *Five and Seven Palm Row*. The sixth dwelling is located on the north side of Palm Row and uses the *123 Cordova* address, although number *Six Palm Row* can be seen on the Palm Row entrance. The buildings share a common green.

By 1907 the Palm Row residences were occupied and Mr. Ammidown maintained ownership of the rental properties until his death in 1913. Early renters of the houses included a pharmacist, a physician, a Florida East Coast Railway Station official, a clothier, a merchant, and an architect. After Mr. Ammidown's death in 1913, the houses were inherited by his nephew, Philip Holmes Ammidown, who died the following year and left the real estate to his son, another Henry Philip Ammidown. During the period, the short street combined residences and businesses quite easily. Dr. G. A. Davies moved to the home in 1911. By 1917, the property had become the Beckley School for Boys and Girls and in the early 1920s it became the Palm Row School and Kindergarten with Mrs. Myrtie Warren Felkel as principal. At the time, her husband, Herbert Felkel, was editor of the *St. Augustine Record*.

The centrally located building, *Three–Four Palm Row*, functioned as a duplex for years. In the early 1930s, Vera Bacon operated a beauty shop at *Three Palm Row*. The law offices of Martz and McClure occupied the building in the early 1980s. Paul Martz was elected city commissioner in 1970, George McClure was elected Mayor of St.

Augustine Beach in 1980. Now listed only as Three Palm Row, the building contains professional offices. Claude C. Speer, a partner in the drug store located at *One Palm Row* lived at *Five Palm Row*. Following Mr. Speer's occupancy, the house was converted into two apartments with *5–1/2 Palm Row* listed in the 1918 City Directory as the home of J. D. Rahner, general passenger agent of the Florida East Coast Railway. His portion of the house was later occupied by photographer Harry M. Wolf. The first occupant of *Six Palm Row* was Fred R. Allen, a merchant and farmer. The house was purchased in 1941 by J. J. Brown and has been a family home since then. One of the earliest renters of *Seven Palm Row* was R. Fuller Callaway, president of the Callaway Clothing Company. For a time it was rented by Minerva E. Muir who operated Muir's Chinese Shop. Although residents have changed, and the paint is peeling on a few homes, Palm Row remains a lovely thoroughfare between St. George and Cordova streets.

St. George Street

St. George Street has a rare ambiance that makes it easy to appreciate how residents of America's First City live, preserve, and enjoy their heritage. The next several houses are examples of the architectural diversity of the area.

The Gingerbread House

Nestled between the Palm Row houses and Villa Flora is St. Augustine's most ornate surviving example of Civil War era Carpenter Gothic architecture. The Gingerbread House at *232 St. George Street* drips sawn wood ornamentation from the eaves. A balcony and gable dormers provide accents with a finial and diamond shaped multipane windows adding embellishment. The house was purchased in 1873 by J. Downing Stanbury and was occupied for the next half century by members of his family. Mr. Stanbury was the official surveyor for St. Johns County, Justice of the Peace, Notary Public, attorney, and County Treasurer. In 1941 Mr. and Mrs. Henry Gibson bought the house and operated it as the Magnolia Inn until 1945. In recent years it has again become a private residence and has been magnificently restored.

Villa Flora

In 1894, Baptist minister A. O. Weenolsen and his wife purchased a large lot extending from St. George Street to Cordova Street. There were four structures on it. The Weenolsens, winter residents from Minneapolis, Minnesota, bought the property from Mrs. Gertrude Solomon, widow of Max Bloomfield who had published *Bloomfield's Guide to St. Augustine* in 1883.

The Weenolsens built Villa Flora at *234 St. George Street* in 1898. The "Estate of Flowers" is an architectural gem. It was one of the first in the city to use yellow–brown bricks instead of the more conventional red brick. Its style combines Moorish Revival and Romanesque elements with unusual touches, including the most extensive stained glass in any surviving residential building in St. Augustine. During 1899 the Weenolsens added a verandah. A walkway, later called Flora Promenade, was constructed between Cordova and St. George streets with a coquina gateway on the Cordova side. There is a broad, imposing flight of stairs leading to the main floor. The two–story house had a three–story flat tower. The massive porch base was built of coquina, still a popular building material at the turn of the century. Upstairs were two brown–brick fireplaces: one with a marble mantle. A sun parlor was added to the residence. An article in 1899 from the society newspaper, *Tatler*, called the house "One of the most attractive and artistic homes in the city... surrounded by grounds brilliant with roses and flowers, shaded by stately palms."

Villa Flora, built 1898

The Weenolsens realized the value of the other structures on the property which included a one–story house facing Cordova, a two–story house facing St. George Street, a one–story office, and a one–story outbuilding. Small, cozy dwellings became popular around the turn of the century. Northerners came to St. Augustine and the Weenolsens became landlords. The two–story structure was moved to the rear of the lot when construction of Villa Flora began in 1898. The one–story cottage on Cordova Street, which the Weenolsens had previously occupied and remodeled, was retained and used for rentals. In 1900 the two buildings were connected by contractor William Fishwick and shortly after another cottage, the Hermitage, was built. The unpretentious winter residences were occupied by numerous North-erners. An author, Edwin Asa Dix, from East Orange, New Jersey, and his wife Marion wintered in one of the bungalows in 1901 and 1902. Mr. Dix was a contributor to *Century* magazine. Henry M. Hill, editor and owner of the Bridgeport, Connecticut *Evening Post* and his wife also rented a cottage.

In 1906 the Weenolsens sold the home to Alanson Wood. Following Mr. Wood's death, which occurred soon after the transac-tion, his widow Bessie and daughter, Lucy J. Lewis acquired the property. Mrs. Wood purchased her daughter's share and operated the buildings as a hotel through the 1920s. She also ran the Wander In gift shop, located in the building. In 1934, Ruth Masters, daughter of mayor and city manager Eugene Masters, operated the Villa Flora Grill from the premises.

During the 1940s, the Sisters of St. Joseph acquired the prop-erty. Used as an adjunct to the academy, the building served for years as classroom space and a kindergarten center. In 1973, Villa Flora and the annex, Brown Hall, were returned to residential use. The Sisters of St. Joseph converted it for use as a House of Formation, or Novitiate, which serves as home and training center for young girls wishing to enter the order. The tower room is now used as a chapel. The annex has been carefully coordinated with the architectural quality of the 1898 building. The Sisters handmade hundreds of tessellated tiles to match existing tiles and used them to create an outdoor Florida room. The old coquina gate from the Flora Promenade still stands on *Cordova Street* and one of the town's original gas lights remains beside the walkway.

Bronson Cottage

Andrew Jackson Davis was one of the most influential architects practicing in America in the decades before the Civil War. He was commissioned to create numerous state capitols and is perhaps best remembered for his Gothic Revival designs. The only known example of his work in Florida is located at *252 St. George Street*. It was designed in 1875 as a winter home for Robert and Isabel Donaldson Bronson, the recently married son and daughter of two of Davis' old friends and clients. Mrs. Bronson asked him to design a "simple, inexpensive cottage home" to be built for about $5,000. Mr. Davis obliged them with several working drawings which, with a few modifications, were used by local builders. The Bronsons wintered in the cottage for several years, rented it, and finally sold it in 1905. In later years, the Bronson Cottage was used as a Fine Arts Building by St. Joseph Academy. In 1988 the Sisters sold the house to a private owner who is now restoring it.

Colonel Upham's Winter Cottage

As the "Winter Newport" of late 19th–century America, St. Augustine served as a mecca for many socially and financially prominent families. During the late Victorian period Lieutenant Colonel John J. Upham came to town, attracted by the growing reputation of resort

hotels being built by Henry Morrison Flagler. A career service officer and Milwaukee bachelor, Colonel Upham spent part of 1891 at the Alcazar Hotel enjoying St. Augustine's social life. He returned the following year, having married and been promoted to full colonel.

Colonel Upham's Winter Cottage, built 1892

The Uphams retired after he completed 30 years of military service. They chose to make St. Augustine their permanent winter home.

In October 1892 Caroline and John Upham purchased the lot at *268 St. George Street* and began supervising construction of a house of their own design. The lot the Uphams purchased lay directly south of the First Presbyterian Church. The land was originally acquired by a New Yorker, John P. Howard, after the Civil War and in 1880 was conveyed to Amos C. Spear. Mr. Spear, who was related to Mr. Howard by marriage, was from Burlington, Vermont, and had considerable land holdings in St. Augustine. In 1886 he sold the St. George Street lot as well as other properties to Curtis A. Hibbard, also from Burlington, who worked with the St. Augustine dry goods firm of Sabin, Abbott, and Company. It was through Mr. Hibbard that Colonel Upham acquired the lot.

Construction began on the walls of the Upham house in late 1892. The 12–room plan was described in a *Florida Times–Union* report as follows:" A large room (rectangular) is wedged open in the rear to the center, so that each side of the wedge will be a spacious room, a sort of dove–tailed shaped foundation, thus gaining an additional room and catching the sun from all quarters of the compass. The wedge–shaped space is converted into a conservatory, no two rooms being alike. Everything will be of the best known to modern improvements. The location was selected because the street is paved." Another feature of the unusual house was a large fireplace angled toward three rooms.

A touch of mystery and tragedy is associated with the construction of the house. The builder, John T. Lander, mysteriously vanished in January 1893 after issuing instructions to his workers. A manhunt was organized to search for the well–respected resident; however, the unsuccessful attempt was finally abandoned. In mid–February, his body was found on an Anastasia Island beach. A coroner's jury rendered a verdict of accidental drowning. In order to dispel any further rumors, a plausible explanation was devised stating that Mr. Lander was traveling to North Beach in search of a man who could assist him in hoisting a boiler. While on the trestle of the bridge, it was said, he slipped and plunged into the North River. His body was carried out to sea and finally washed onto shore at high tide weeks later. With that, the mystery came to an end—and the truth remained hidden.

Despite the taint of tragedy, the new home rose rapidly. A housewarming in 1894 provided an opportunity to use the centrally located fireplace, around which the entire party danced in circular formation. The Uphams, part of St. Augustine society, entertained frequently. Mrs. Henry M. Flagler attended a tea in 1894. Mrs. William Deering was a guest at a ball a few years later. R. G. Dun of the New York financial firm, Dun and Bradstreet, visited in 1893. Mrs. Bertson James, sister–in–law of novelist Henry James and psychologist William James visited frequently. Journalist Clark Howell, editor of the *Atlanta Constitution*, was a guest at a reception for Mrs. James in 1895.

Sanborn Fire Insurance maps of the period provide a clear picture of many alterations. Between 1893 and 1899 a one–story rear section was raised to two–stories and topped with a skylight. An iron water tank shown on the north side of the house in 1893 was replaced by a two–story addition. A one–story ell was extended southward from the rear section of the house and covered with a glass roof. The front porch was also altered during the early years. It was extended and a second–story section was added on the front. Colonel Upham died in 1898 in Milwaukee. Although Mrs. Upham maintained ownership of the house until 1915, she frequently rented it to other winter visitors.

The Upham house was built at a time when luxury and elegance were a central part of the life–style for St. Augustine's wealthy winter residents. The home has been preserved and continues to add to the charm of the Ancient City. For a time between 1955 and 1970, it was used as an apartment house . In 1970 it was restored to its original form as a single family residence and later was converted to include apartments again.

The house has been magnificently restored. It retains many of the distinctive Queen Anne features such as jigsawn rafters and brackets, turned wood posts, and novelty shingles. The porch has a Chinese Chippendale appearance and lattice work ornamentation in the gables add an attractive touch. Additions over the years have resulted in a basic octagonal shape, probably quite different from the original Upham design. Nevertheless, the winter cottage on St. George Street remains one of St. Augustine's attractive and interesting homes.

Buena Esperanza's Victorian Homes

Buena Esperanza means Good Hope. In the 18th century a small mission church was built in the area to serve the spiritual needs of the Pocotalaca Indians who lived along Maria Sanchez Creek, including present day Oneida Street. During the second Spanish period Bernardo Segui, a Minorcan merchant, acquired the Buena Esperanza property and developed one of Florida's first commercial orange groves.

Mr. Segui arrived in St. Augustine as a penniless survivor of the New Smyrna colony. He became one of the wealthiest merchants in St. Augustine and lived in a two–story home on what was then Hospital Street. Sr. Segui purchased the house, now known as the Segui–Kirby Smith House, at *12 Avilés Street* in 1786. It was left to his widow Aguada when he died in 1813. In 1821 she leased it to Judge Joseph Lee Smith, the first federal judge in the new territory of Florida. Judge Smith's son was Confederate General Edmund Kirby Smith. By 1830, Augustus Poujaud, a Frenchman who had married a St. Augustine woman, Maria Mauricia Sanchez, a descendant of one of the first Spanish period families, encouraged residential development of the area. He was unsuccessful.

It was not until 1885 that a workable plan emerged for Buena Esperanza's residential development. At that time, the St. Augustine Improvement Company, a local real estate development firm, purchased and subdivided the Buena Esperanza tract. By 1894 more than 30 large houses lined *Oneida, South, Central, Cerro, and Blanco streets.* The Buena Esperanza area developed into one of St. Augustine's outstanding Victorian neighborhoods.

Two grand estates of Buena Esperanza, sharing similar histories, lie secluded behind dense foliage at the end of Oneida Street. Both homes were built for officials of the St. Augustine Improvement Company: President Heth Canfield and Vice President George Atwood, Jr.

Three Oaks

Three Oaks, at *175 Oneida Street*, was built for Mr. Atwood in 1890 and, not surprisingly, the two-and-a-half story wood frame building has a concrete block veneer over the wood. The St. Augustine Improvement Company manufactured its own "improved concrete veneer." He added an individual touch by setting stones in the veneer in patterns of alternating sizes. The house has undergone numerous alterations over the decades.

An 1894 birds-eye view of the city shows that the house had a gabled roof. At that time there were no porches or balconies. Around 1910, the residence had acquired a distinctive roofline, this time a steeply pitched hip roof with two levels of balconies. The house reached its present appearance after renovations following a fire in the 1960s. Distinctive architectural elements include Tuscan arches on the porch, cast concrete trim accents on the doors and windows and a raised basement, one of the few in the city.

Mr. Atwood, Jr. was no stranger to St. Augustine. His father had come to the city during the Civil War. In addition to overseeing the development of his orange groves, Mr. Atwood, Sr. became prominent in the Radical Republican Party. He was appointed County Clerk and Clerk of the Circuit Court in St. Johns County in 1869 and died in the 1880s.

It was only after his father's death that Mr. Atwood, Jr. became active in the St. Augustine Improvement Company. He was a noted sportsman who served as president of the Polo Club in 1895. He also enjoyed riding horseback along the seawall. In 1934, State Senator A. M. Taylor told the *St. Augustine Record* that Mr. Atwood, Jr. had won a wager by riding along the seawall, around the Fort, and onto the nearby grounds of the San Marco Hotel. Not content with that, he urged his mount up the more than 20–step staircase, through the main hall of the hotel, into the bar on the second story, and ordered a drink.

The drink was said to have been served by an open–mouthed bartender. Senator Taylor also remembered Mr. Atwood, Jr. as the leader of a St. Augustine club, the Tall Sluggers of the Saint Sebastians. The club's members met at the only saloon in town, a bar located on Charlotte Street around the corner from Cathedral Place.

In 1893, Mr. Atwood, Jr. sold Three Oaks to Wheeler Stevens, a wealthy wholesale grocer from Zanesville, Ohio. The Stevens' two daughters and a niece entertained often. *Tatler* frequently reported lively activities at the estate. One of the Stevens girls, Anne, inherited Three Oaks around the turn of the century. She and her husband, William A. Knight, continued the tradition of hospitality. While living at Three Oaks, Mr. Knight served as president and secretary–treasurer of the St. Augustine Country Club which was situated on the south end of Oneida Street. A local resident remembers the Knight family's numerous dance recitals and maypole celebrations held in the garden. Children also performed for their elders in the ballroom on the top floor of the house, bicycled in circles around a fountain on the property, and attended school in a remodeled garage. Mrs. Knight cultivated roses and ferns which filled the garden. The family frequently took boat rides from the dock and delighted St. Augustine residents with their new purchase, one of the first automobiles in the city. During the 1930s, one of the Knight daughters married T. Rogero Mickler, a local attorney and mayor of St. Augustine. The home remained in the family until around 1950 when Mrs. Knight sold it shortly after her husband's death.

The charm of Three Oaks in the Victorian era was captured on film when actresses Billie Burke and Ethel Barrymore starred in movies made on the estate's grounds.

Three Oaks after remodeling

Charles Usina bought the property in 1954. The son of a local cigar manufacturer, he had served in the Florida House of Representatives in 1944 and from 1947 until his death in 1966. His widow Phyllis, a reporter for the *St. Augustine Record*, sold the property in 1967. In the late 1960s, Three Oaks was acquired by German partners, Alfons Bernhard and John Bernworth. When Mr. Bernworth died in 1979, Three Oaks was sold. The new owner and his wife had been friends of Messrs. Bernhard and Bernworth. The interior of the house was completely modified, except for the hardwood floors, an impressive staircase, and the trademark tiles the German partners had installed. Bathrooms were added, bedrooms were expanded, and a breakfast room, kitchen additions, and sunroom became part of the modernization. Exterior changes included adding awnings and a porch. The new owners changed the name to Casa Guadalupe because the former owners had installed a tile honoring Our Lady of Guadalupe on the house and placed a statue of her on the lawn. They felt the name change reflected the previous owners' beliefs and interests.

Villa Rosa

Villa Rosa was built in 1895 for Heth Canfield. In the early days, the two–story dwelling had an open tower rising from the center portion of the house. A porte cochere extended over the curved driveway and formal gardens were filled with tropical plants. The wood shingle siding had a natural finish and the windows had blinds with movable louvers, then a novelty.

In 1901 the property was sold to Alfred Jerome Weston, a Yonkers, New York, native who remodeled the home and entertained lavishly. Magnificent interior photographs show gaslight chandeliers, Victorian furnishings, and Oriental ornamentation. An old floor plan of the house showed a first floor consisting of a living room, reception room, library, dining room, kitchen, pantry, buttery, boiler room, bath, and three porches. The second floor had five bedrooms, three baths, a sleeping porch, and an open porch. The grounds also included a servant's cottage, garage, boathouse, and long dock where the early owners kept their yacht. Distinctive artificial stone pillars with the name Villa Rosa inscribed still stand at the north and south ends of the driveway.

The Weston family maintained the estate as a winter home until 1935 when it was sold to the Sisters of Resurrection, an Episcopal order established in St. Augustine during the Flagler era. The Sisters of Resurrection used Villa Rosa as a convent. One of the members of the order, Sister Esther Carlotta, was the daughter of General Robert E. Lee's personal physician. She operated a rest home and served as president of the Anna Dummett Chapter of the Daughters of the Confederacy. When she died at Villa Rosa in the 1940s, the property was willed to the Episcopal Church whose members operated the house as a rest home, called Resthaven, for about 15 years. In the late 1960s, Villa Rosa was acquired by German partners, Alfons Bernhard and John Bernworth. Since their death the building has remained vacant and is in sad need of repair.

One of the finest examples of Victorian architecture in Buena Esperanza is the two-story house at *160 Martin Luther King Avenue.* Turned spindle posts, a frieze, and gingerbread trim decorate the porch. A jigsawn balustrade displays a touch of Moorish Revival influence and the gable has jigsawn rafters and brackets. The house was originally owned by George Old of the St. Augustine Gas Company.

Through continuing restoration efforts, many of the older houses south of King Street have been preserved. With continued attention, the neighborhood retains its architectural significance and remains a proud example of the architectural heritage of the city.

Lincolnville

Africa was the first name chosen for the new black community that developed south of King Street after the Civil War. The settlement began on the banks of Maria Sanchez Creek and gradually spread west. The various subdivisions and developments that arose on the southwest peninsula later became known collectively as Lincolnville. St.

Augustine was atypical in that it never followed the post-Civil War pattern of development in other cities which led to one predominately black section of town. From the earliest years, black neighborhoods have been scattered throughout the city. Within this section of the book, the emphasis is on Lincolnville.

Lincolnville as it is known today is comprised of several small subdivisions generally named for their developers. Dumas Tract lies just south of Bridge Street and is the genesis of the Lincolnville community. The subdivision evolved out of early 19th century Spanish lands granted to Bartolo Juarez and Gaspar Papy. Developed initially as orange groves, the land later became speculative property and was eventually acquired by Philip Weedman and Peter Dumas. Mr. Dumas, a county clerk and post-Civil War leader of the Florida Radical Republicans, owned the land when blacks first sought property for a settlement after the Civil War.

Washington Street

Houses arose on Oneida and Bridge streets during the late 1870s and by 1885 the Dumas Tract along Washington Street was a rapidly growing community. Between 1885 and 1894 the Maria Sanchez Creek was filled in for construction of the Flagler buildings. Commercial structures sprouted along Washington Street. As the "main street" of Lincolnville it combined businesses, residences, churches, and entertainment spots. Some of the city's few commercial Victorian buildings exist along Washington Street. The few surviving porches and overhangs on the street are reminiscent of days gone by.

One of the oldest buildings on the block is a one-story frame building at *93 Washington Street*. Built between 1865 and 1885, the little structure was once a neighborhood meeting place and was later rented by E. Aldrich Johnson, a funeral director. In the 1920s it was known as Temperance Hall. It then became a tavern and is currently vacant. Another night spot was the Lincolnville Bar at *83 Washington Street*. Since its construction between 1904 and 1910, the one-story masonry building has served as a saloon, store, poolroom, and meeting place for the Iroquois Social Club. A tile floor and massive ornate liquor shelf are two distinctive interior characteristics. In 1979 the Lincolnville Jazz Band performed for several nights in an effort to promote restoration enthusiasm for Washington Street and the Lincolnville neighborhood. The concert became an annual event growing to the point it could no longer be contained on narrow Washington Street. The early November two-day festival moved to a large open area at the south end of Riberia Street. Funds generated by the festival are channeled through a restoration committee seeking to improve the historic area.

One partially restored building on the block is the Odd Fellows Hall at 92 Washington Street. The three-story masonry structure was built in 1908 and has served as a meeting place since that time. The first floor has been a movie theater, an office for physician Dr. Thomas G. Freeland, and a grocery store. In 1980 some restoration was made to the stucco finish. Unfortunately, the original interesting two-story open porch is gone and the house still requires a great deal of care. The first floor is used as a meeting place for the owners, San Sebastian Lodge Number 3117. The home at 70 Washington Street has been beautifully restored and now serves as a soup kitchen. It is hoped that others on the historic street can also receive the care they need.

Many other interesting buildings appear in Lincolnville. Old St. Joseph's School, located at 79 Sanford Street, is the oldest surviving black school building and one of the oldest brick buildings in the city. Also called St. Benedict the Moor School, the building housed classrooms for black students from 1898 into the mid-1900s. The school, operated by the Catholic Church, followed the tradition of the Sisters of St. Joseph and evolved through the efforts of two St. Augustine women. Mlle. Stella Dumas, the daughter of Peter B. Dumas, deeded the Dumas Block (bordered by Central Avenue, Sanford, St. Francis, and De Haven Streets) to Bishop Moore in 1890. Mother Catherine Drexel who came from a wealthy Philadelphia family contributed the bulk of the construction expense of the building. The old school housed the headquarters for the Northeast Florida Community Action Agency for a few years in the late 1970s and early 1980s.

St. Benedict the Moor Catholic Church at 82 Central Avenue was also constructed on the Dumas Block. It is a fine Mediterranean Revival

structure built between 1909 and 1911. The mission parapet and ornate stained glass windows blend with the Victorian elements. The church is one of the oldest African-American Catholic churches in Florida.

An example of some of the fine Victorian structures in the Dumas Tract can be seen at *89 Bridge Street.* Constructed between 1871 and 1885, the two-story residence has ornate jigsawn carved brackets and porch railings on a two-story open porch.

Detail, 89 Bridge Street, photograph 1980

One of the residents was Carrie Macon, a black woman who owned and operated a hair styling shop at *161-1/2 St. George Street.* The steeple of Trinity Methodist Church is a visible landmark along Bridge Street. Constructed in 1913, the masonry building faces Lincolnville and represents a continuity of the Methodist religion in St. Augustine which, for a time, was maintained by an exclusively black congregation.

Genovar Tract

Another early residential area in Lincolnville was the Genovar Tract which is located along *Kings Ferry Road and Lincoln Street.* It is named for then-prominent merchant, Bartolo Genovar, who purchased and sub-divided the tract by 1878. Small homes lined the two principal streets by 1885 and subsequent development has generally been by blacks. An example of the Victorian architecture can be seen at *104 Lincoln Street* where the home exhibits chamfered posts and jigsawn brackets.

A subdivision lying between Dumas and Genovar Tracts has been assigned the name Atwood for Anna and George Atwood. The tract corresponds to a 1792 land grant to Martin Hernandez, a Minorcan carpenter. The land was conveyed to Jose Mariano Hernandez, a politician, land owner, and military officer. The Atwoods purchased the land in 1865 and sold it in 1887 to the St. Augustine Improvement Company.

Keith Subdivision

Number *55 Keith Street* contains one wing of the original plantation house. The most significant structure in Keith subdivision is St. Cyprians Episcopal Church at *279 Lovett Street*. Constructed in 1900, the attractive building consists of a gabled tower, multi-diamond and stained glass windows, pilasters, and various Victorian elements.

In 1885, as the African-American communities were growing, half of the working population were employed in such jobs as carpenters, bakers, butchers, shoemakers, and laborers. The directory of the time lists one teacher, four ministers, store clerks, restaurant operators, and a grocer. Two men held government positions: F. E. Witsell was customs collector and John Papino was town marshall. In 1889 Domingo M. Pappy was justice of the peace and a restaurant owner. In later years, Mrs. Pappy was grocer and operated an employment service for blacks. During the 1880s African-Americans held a few political positions. During the late 1880s and into the 1890s poll taxes and complicated ballot box laws made it difficult for them to participate in and grow with the local governmental forces. Throughout the Flagler era, African-Americans were encouraged to provide entertainment for the wealthy winter residents. By the early 1900s, many were employed by the railroad. The Afro-American Insurance Company and Union Burial League were established.

African-American-operated businesses in the 1920s and 1930s included: the Home Circle Publishing Company where James Reddick was editor; the Sanitary House Cleaning Company, owned by the Welters brothers; the Iceberg Ice Cream Company owned by Forward and DeLarge; and the West Side Dry Cleaning Company owned by Boyd W. Smith. In recent years, two of St. Augustine's black educators have been honored. The Richard J. Murray and James A. Webster schools commemorate these men. Frank B. Butler (1885-1973) operated the Palace Market on Washington Street and was president of College Park Realty Company. In 1927 the black businessman began buying property 10 miles southeast of St. Augustine on Anastasia Island. He donated the land, which extends from the beach to the Intercoastal Waterway, to the county for use as a recreational area for African-Americans. It is named Butler Beach in his honor.

Frank B. Butler and his daughter Minnie Mae
in Palace Market on Washington Street, ca. 1920s

Like many other areas south of King Street, there is increasing interest in preserving the historic buildings remaining and restoring them carefully. At present, a number of Lincolnville's early structures are being turned into private residences again.

Although we have commented briefly on the Abbott Tract and the area north of the Castillo de San Marcos, the emphasis of the book now turns to the early statehood era and the increasing development which occurred in that neighborhood.

Chapter 4
Abbott Tract

First Spanish Period, 1565-1763
British Decades, 1763-1784
Second Spanish Period, 1784–1821
Territorial Era, 1821-1845

Early Statehood, 1845-1888

Flagler Golden Era, 1888-1914
Twentieth Century, 1914-present

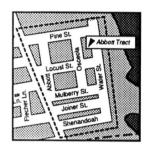

During the early part of the 18th century, the land north of the Walled City was occupied by Macariz Indians. By 1757, a group of Canary Islanders had settled in the north area of St. Augustine as part of the Spanish empire's strategy to populate the new colonies. By the British occupation, land grants were given and homesteads were established on what was then outlying acreage. The early settlements were eventually abandoned, thereby leaving the sparsely populated area ripe for development. The first part of the outlying acreage to realize extensive, permanent growth was on property just north of the Castillo de San Marcos. Now known as the Abbott Tract, the area has matured over the years. Rich in history, the section sparkles with architectural gems and has the largest concentration of 19th century structures in the city.

Spanish Land Grants

Abbott Tract evolved from five early 19th century Spanish land grants and from land made available for new Florida residents during the Territorial era. The five parcels lay within St. Augustine's outer defense perimeter, the Mil y Quinientas. The first strip of land, adjoining the northern border of the Castillo de San Marcos, was acquired in 1803 by Jose Noda who came to St. Augustine from the Canary Islands. North of his land lay the property of Jose Garcia, a freedman whose property was later purchased by Sr. Noda. By the late 1830s the consolidated grants were known as the Noda Concession. Next to the Noda Concession was the property which Juan Genopoly farmed. Adjacent to his grant was that of Pedro Estopa, a farmer from Minorca who probably occupied the property some years before its legal acquisition in 1807. Sr. Estopa's northern neighbor was another Minorcan, Juan Villalonga. In 1807 he received 341 acres, one of the largest of the Mil y Quinientas grants.

The southernmost portion of the land, the Noda Concession, was the first to be divided for residential development. Sr. Noda sold the land in 1838 to General Peter Sken (Skenandoah) Smith, a New Yorker who came to St. Augustine for health reasons. He was part of the first wave of Northerners who came to the city seeking cures for congestive and respiratory problems including bronchitis and tuberculosis. Mr. Smith, a unique St. Augustine resident, was a land speculator and more. He published a newspaper, the *St. Augustine News*, in order to respond to Elias B. Gould, then publisher of the *East Florida Herald*, who was General Smith's most ardent adversary. The two men fought about many things, including the construction of canals and railways across St. Johns County, with Mr. Gould accusing General Smith of seeking material gain. When the two opposed each other in a state legislative race, Mr. Gould won by 71 of the 311 votes cast. The animosity extended far beyond political differences. As an elder of the local Presbyterian church, Mr. Gould resisted the General's inclusion into the church's governing body. General Smith was granted the prestigious position and later managed to oust Mr. Gould from leadership.

North City

Within a year after purchasing the Noda Concession, General Smith divided it into blocks and lots for resale. The subdivision, soon called North City, extended from Clinch Street, now the northern strip of the Fort Green, north to Joiner Street. The subdivision ran from the North River marshes on the east side to the western border of Shell Road, now called San Marco Avenue. Clinch Street, created by General Smith out of confusion about Noda's southern boundary, reverted to federal ownership in the early 20th century and ceased to function as a thoroughfare. Two of the first sales in North City were to his business partners, William H. Simmons and John C. Cleland. The men bought a two–block area east of Water Street between Shenandoah and Joiner Streets. It is interesting to note that Joiner Street was named for land developer Joshua Joyner, but spelled incorrectly as were many streets, including Shenandoah, originally named for Peter Skenandoah Smith.

Mr. Cleland, the district attorney, made great efforts to develop the North City property. In 1839 he built Beach Cottage, which will be discussed shortly. Between 1839 and 1844, he developed the North City Wharf Company and a steam saw mill which were located between Clinch and Shenandoah streets, near the waterfront. Both buildings were probably destroyed in the late 1940s after the companies went bankrupt. The North City Hotel on *Shell Road* between *Shenandoah and Joiner streets* was also built under Mr. Cleland's direction around 1843, as were several one– and two–story dwellings which were the products of the combined imaginations of Mr. Cleland and General Smith. Of these early residences, two remain: the Cleland Mansion at *23 Water Street* and a small house at *19 Joiner Street*. Both are excellent examples of St. Augustine's Territorial Period architecture.

Davis Range was the name associated with the land north of the Noda Concession. During the 1820s and 1830s, Mary Ann and William Davis consolidated lands formerly comprising the Spanish grants of Juan Genopoly, Pedro Estropa, and Juan Villalonga. In 1839 the Davis' newly surveyed property consisted of 130 lots. The subdivision extended north along Shell Road from Joiner Street to a point 150 feet beyond Pine Street. The majority of the houses were built between Joiner and Mulberry streets. Davis Range sales never matched the success of the popular Noda Concession real estate development. By the mid–1840s, Davis Range and the Noda Concession fell victim to economic depression and repercussions from the on–going Seminole wars. The conflicts between the Seminole Indians and the U.S. settlers escalated in 1835 and lasted through the mid–1840s. The wars disrupted staple agriculture in nearby areas forcing settlers to abandon farms and leave the state. Winter visitors were cautioned against coming to Florida. Some citizens sympathized with the Indians, others fought them during the uneasy times.

From roughly 1845 until the end of the Civil War, North City remained basically unchanged. The Davis property was purchased by Mary and William Van Ness in 1877. Mr. Van Ness, a former Union Army officer, participated in reconstruction politics as chairman of the Constitutional Union Party Convention which met in Tallahassee, Florida, in September 1867. The following year he served as mayor of St. Augustine. For a time the family lived in Beach Cottage and then moved to Jacksonville.

Abbott Tract

In 1860 Lucy Abbott was a young woman in her 20s when she arrived in St. Augustine from Charleston, South Carolina. She began purchasing land north of the Castillo de San Marcos. By the 1870s the astute business woman owned a large tract of land north of the city. She purchased the Noda Concession as well as land up to and including lots on the north side of Locust Street. She built nine structures in the area which still stand. The first house dates from 1861, the last several from between 1885 and 1894. Besides abutting the historic Spanish Fort, Abbott Tract also lies just south of the Mission of Nombre de Dios. The eastern boundary slips gently into marshlands overlooking Matanzas Bay and the old Shell Road forms the western rim. Rapid development in the area continued until around 1904 when 126 houses lined the streets. Fewer than 20 were from the pre–Civil War era. By 1923 the Davis Range and Noda tracts became collectively known as Abbott Tract.

Abbott House

Number 22 *Water Street* was built around 1861 by Miss Abbott's uncle, Captain John W. Starke, who lived in the house until the Civil War when it became a hospital. It was said that blood stains remained on the parlor floor well into the 1930s. When the hospital was finally moved to the St. Francis Barracks on Marine Street, the house was rented. The gracious southern home became Miss Abbott's residence in 1873 and was her primary residence until her death in 1919.

An early sketch of the house exists. From 1875 to 1878, about 70 western plains Indians were incarcerated at Fort Marion, *Zotom's Sketch of Abbott House, ca. 1875-78* the name the Territorial government had given to the Castillo de San Marcos. Zotom, one of the captured Kiowa Indians, sketched the Abbott House from a western vantage. He showed a two–story structure in an L–shaped configuration with an open porch on the north side, gabled roofs, three chimneys, and a picket fence enclosing the property.

Over the next 20 years, several changes occurred. The bird's–eye views of 1885 and 1894 show a hip roof rather than a gabled roof. By 1910 an east wing with two two–story porches had been added. A map of 1910 showed a three–story tower rising alongside the western porch; however, the tower did not appear on later maps. In 1933 author and critic, Van Wyck Brooks occupied the house. He wrote to his friend, author Lewis Mumford, telling of his joy at being in the quaint southern town and describing the residence as a huge southern house with great airy bedrooms ten paces long. He commented that the "upstairs balconies at front and rear, overlooking a half–acre of forsaken garden, filled with palm and orange trees, with an old Spanish Fort just beyond, and the ocean beyond that and overall a vast magnolia tree, in leaf and almost in blossom that covers us like an umbrella."

The interesting residence has a charm that contributes to Water Street's ambience. The east porch nestles into the L of the east wing and main section and is adorned by Neo–Classical balustrades, jigsawn brackets, and chamfered posts. The brackets are intricately cut to display a four–point star inside a circle with a graceful swirl extension accented by an acorn drop. Around 1953 the house was purchased by Frank Tart who had served as mayor in 1944 and 1945.

Beach Cottage

Concealed within the walls of the stately Queen Anne residence at 23 *Water Street* is a simpler structure once called the Beach Cottage. A construction date of 1839 was supplied by the *Southern Democrat* when it mentioned the "mansion, Beach Cottage" in a July issue of that year. The date confers a distinction upon the house–that of being one of the few remaining examples of Territorial period architecture still standing in St. Augustine. The cottage was sited on a choice lot overlooking the Fort Green and waterfront. The two–story wood frame residence later evolved into the larger Victorian structure.

A sketch in *Chapin's St. Augustine Directory of 1885–1886* indicates the existing rectangular building once had a one–story porch, supported by round posts, a style typical of the period. Several large windows or doors opened onto the porch roof which was enclosed by a railing. There was a matching railing across the second–story roof. The original Beach Cottage faced south. The Shenandoah Street door opens inches from the western wall of the old structure. The spacious living room of the existing home contains virtually all the first floor area of J. C. Cleland's original cottage. A view from the water side reveals a gable centered over the rectangular shape.

Beach Cottage, ca. 1885

In 1854 Trinity Episcopal Church acquired the property to provide a home for the minister, the Reverend Alfred A. Miller and his wife Catherine. After Reverend Miller's death, his widow purchased the house and later sold it to Mary and William Van Ness. The Van Ness family lived in the Beach Cottage until at least 1868. In 1869 when the family moved to Jacksonville an article in the local paper emphasized that Mr. Van Ness "offers his place for sale at a very low price. It is one of the most desirable residences in the South." Around 1892, R. W. Nesbitt, roadmaster for the Jacksonville, St. Augustine, and Halifax River Railroad, married Margaret Perry and bought the Beach Cottage property. The new Mrs. Nesbitt, already a Water Street resident, was a descendent of the Minorcan Capo family who had migrated from New Smyrna in 1777. The Nesbitts did the first extensive alteration of the property. Inspection of the old house tells an interesting story. An intersecting gable roof visible in the attic indicates the addition of a northwest–oriented wing. The condition of the shingles on the older roof gave evidence of only three or four years of exposure to the elements after which time a new roof and additional remodeling were undertaken. An external view from the western vantage shows a symmetrical structure excluding a portion of the northern wing, probably Nesbitt's addition before a second remodeling took place.

In 1895 William Deering bought the property. He was a wealthy businessman who had established the Deering Harvester Company in 1893. The company later merged with a similar business to create International Harvester where his sons, Charles and James, served as officers. The senior Mr. Deering added to the northern wing and made other architectural changes to achieve the Queen Anne appearance, thus creating the present stately but irregular shape. The Victorian elements added by Mr. Deering included the pyramid–shaped tower, novelty shingles, a bay, jigsawn bargeboards, turned posts, and bracket work. Sanborn Fire Insurance maps of the period show a wing extension on the north side and a one–story wrap–around porch on the east and south. Later Sanborn maps show that a one–story porch had been enclosed in 1910 and a second story added in 1917. By 1924 a one–story open porch appeared and a small porch on the west side was added. The present appearance includes the front porch, a two–story open porch facing the water, and a one–story porch on the south. The large and elegant structure resulting from the numerous modifications once set the character of the Water Street neighborhood.

Miramar

Miramar, a two–story brick and frame dwelling, was built in 1905. It is located at *21 Water Street*. Architect Fred A. Henderich designed the original frame portion of the house using wood and palm tree posts on the porch. Miramar was built for Walter N. P. Darrow, then a director of the St. Augustine National Bank. After Mr. Darrow's death in 1926, the house remained vacant for almost a decade. For a time in the 1950s and early 1960s, it was occupied by Louise Wise Lewis, a Flagler heiress, and her husband Frederick G. Francis.

Continuing down Water Street, several homes on the south end enhance the elegance prevalent on the tree–shaded thoroughfare. A stately Colonial Revival style residence is located at *33 Water Street*. The two–story frame building was built in 1885 for Roscoe Perry, a Connecticut native who, as a Union soldier, had served in occupied St. Augustine. Mr. Perry returned after the Civil War to marry Margarita Capo, a St. Augustine Minorcan. From 1945 to 1976, the house was occupied by Dr. Adams Clark Walkup, a well–known St. Augustine physician. Across the street at *38 Water Street* is another Colonial Revival residence. Built in the early 1900s, it was the home of Dr. Charles C. Bagwell.

The Lucy Abbott houses, from *42 Water Street* to *56–58 Water Street*, contribute to the character of the street. They exhibit such features as two–story porches, Neo–Classical balustrades, wood scroll trim, and original wood siding. Residents of the houses have included Charles Floyd Hopkins, a descendant of Indian Agent, Gad Humphreys and his wife Isabella Gibbs Hopkins, a descendent of Confederate Army Colonel George Couper Gibbs.

An interesting house at *47 Water Street* evolved from a remodeled portion of a riverfront warehouse. The warehouse, constructed between 1885 and 1894 by Henry A. Boiling was cut in half and moved from the water to the street end of the lot. Two stages of remodeling and one more move resulted in the present appearance and location. During this period, the house was owned by George W. Gibbs and later by his daughter, Rebecca Gibbs Moore. Her son, Harry, remodeled the structure.

There is a large Mediterranean Revival residence at *51 Water Street*. The stucco and brick home was built in 1924 for Harry N. Rodenbaugh, Vice President of Florida East Coast Railway.

One of the oldest brick homes in the city is located at *80 Water Street*. The

80 Water Street, photograph ca . 1910

elegant Queen Anne residence was built around 1890 for bank president John T. Dismukes and was the family residence for over 30 years. Mr. Dismukes established the First National Bank of St. Augustine, the pioneer national bank in the city. He was also president of the Peoples Bank for Savings and was involved in many community projects.

Long before the frame residence at *84 Water Street* was built, it was the site of the first Spanish period Indian church, Nuestra Senora de la Leche. The church was used as a hospital during the British period.

Abbott Mansion

Lucy Abbott's contributions to the development of the subdivision also included the construction of stately Abbott Mansion and the smaller house west of the three–story residence. All were built shortly after 1872. Located at *14 Joiner Street*, the mansion has seen many uses. For a time it was a boarding house, then a convalescent home, and then a guest house. Originally built with a Mansard roof and a two–story, wrap–around porch, the structure dominated the view of North City. In 1922 the mansion again became a single family dwelling when Mary Katherine and Beverley Causey purchased the house.

When he came to St. Augustine, Mr. Causey, a retired New York lawyer, also bought Cord Lumber Company, changing the name to Builders Service Company. The Causeys altered the house from its original Second Empire look to the present Colonial Revival style. A once open porch was replaced by a two–story portico with massive round wooden columns. The Mansard roof was removed and the wood exterior was covered with stucco. When the Causeys moved in 1966, the house was remodeled into apartments and then became a restaurant. Within the past 10 years the home has been remodeled to its former appearance and serves as a private residence.

Castle Warden

A dominant landmark in the area is the Moorish Revival Castle Warden, currently occupied by Ripley's Believe It or Not Museum. The building was constructed in 1887 by the St. Augustine Improvement Company and was the winter residence of William G. Warden, one of Mr. Flagler's and John D. Rockefeller's partners in Standard Oil. The massive structure was the largest poured concrete residence in St. Augustine designed as a private residence. In 1987, Ripley's Believe It or Not Museum added arches to replicate those of the original structure. In 1989 the interior was returned as much as possible to its original state. The building is described in greater detail in the section on Moorish architecture. Note the building to the north of Castle Warden, *15 Shenandoah Street*, was once used as a stable. It was remodeled into a private residence and is now a bed and breakfast inn. It retains Moorish elements and matching battlements atop the stepped gable roof similar to the larger structure.

Within Abbott Tract there is an interesting section of modest dwellings, primarily on the north end of Osceola Street. Property from Locust Street to a few lots beyond Pine Street was purchased in the 1880s and the 1890s for investment purposes. Small, one–story wood frame structures were originally rented to laborers and fishermen. Property owners included Minorcan descendents Mathias Cappellia, Bernard Masters, and C. O. Pomar as well as Edward Vail, Horace Lindsley, John Quigley, and Lucy Plummer. In general, property owners holding land south of Locust Street built and resided in homes on the lots. By 1899, both one– and two–story residences dotted the street, many occupied by descendants of the original colonists.

The western boundary of the Abbott Tract, has been radically altered over the years as commercial encroachment on San Marco Avenue resulted in the demolition or modification of many of the grand old homes that once lined the street. A few early homes have survived. Although *39 San Marco* is dwarfed by a large commercial enterprise, attractive Victorian elements are still visible. Constructed between 1865 and 1885, it was once occupied by the late W. J. Harris, a pioneer photographer and longtime curator of the St. Augustine Historical Society. His images of St. Augustine are preserved at the Historical Society. Another home constructed in the same time frame is located at *41 San Marco Avenue*. The Victorian features of the house include jigsawn rafters, turned gablework, and decorative brackets. The Colonial Revival house at *47 San Marco* has remained a private residence despite the primarily commercial atmosphere. It has been owned by members of the Segui family since 1914. In 1991 the house was purchased from Martha Lee Segui and converted into an inn named Segui House.

Lucy Abbott, St. Augustine's first woman real estate entrepreneur, left a legacy of a beautiful and well-planned city neighborhood. As the decades pass, the sometimes jarring impact of mixed commercial and residential usage seem, at first glance, to have dulled the luster of the old Abbott Tract homes. However, with a bit of time for exploring, prepare to be rewarded by a look at some of the city's architectural gems.

Abbott Tract development was primarily conceived, designed, and developed for residential use. Henry Morrison Flager was soon to arrive in St. Augustine and would build hotels, churches, and homes within the opulent neighborhood he created. As you will see his vision of the Model Land Tract, described in the next chapter, was based on a European model and was executed on a grand scale.

Henry Morrison Flagler
Engraving by J. J. Cade

Chapter 5.
Model Land Tract

First Spanish Period, 1565-1763
British Decades, 1763-1784
Second Spanish Period, 1784–1821
Territorial Era, 1821-1845
Early Statehood, 1845-1888

Flagler's Golden Era, 1888-1914

Twentieth Century, 1914-present

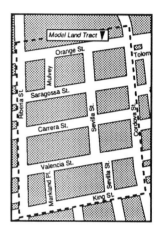

Beyond intrticately carved terra cotta spires rise red and gray towers piercing the air at least 100 feet above the ground. The spires are those of the only Venetian Revival style church in the United States. They overlook Spanish Revival hotel buildings and stately Victorian residences set well back from wide streets. In the 1880s, Henry Morrison Flagler visited St. Augustine and saw the city's potential as a "winter Newport" for wealthy Northerners. As one of the key architects of the expansion of Standard Oil Company, Mr. Flagler's first priority was to create world-class hotels. The vision soon expanded to include churches and an opulent residential area. He began to purchase land that would become the Model Land Tract–an area boundaried by Orange and King streets on the north and south, and Cordova and Riberia streets on the east and west.

Pre-Flagler Era Homes

In 1833 there were only four frame and stone structures on the land. By 1885 three large, elegant homes, as well as some smaller dwellings had been built: Markland estate, Sunnyside House Hotel, the Henry Ball estate, and a smattering of modest structures in the northeastern portion of the property.

The Markland Estate, built by the Dr. and Mrs. Andrew Anderson, is described in Chapter 1. In 1832 Dr. Andrew Anderson purchased strips of land running from Maria Sanchez Creek to the San Sebastian River including extensive holdings bordering King Street on the south and northward to the farmland of Hannah Smith and her son, diplomat–scholar–historian Buckingham Smith.

The Smith property, an 184–foot strip between today's Saragossa and Valencia streets, also stretched from present Cordova Street to the San Sebastian River. It was purchased by Henry Ball, a New Yorker who built his spacious home in the center of the property in 1874. The residence was later moved to the corner of *Sevilla and Carerra streets* and was expanded to become the Barcelona Hotel. The landmark hostelry was razed in 1962.

Two of the older dwellings within today's Model Land Tract quadrangle are found on *Saragossa and Sevilla streets*. The one–story frame house at *13 Saragossa* was built in 1878. It has a catslide roof, reflecting a style common in St. Augustine from 1875 to 1885. St. Augustine's Lopez, Oliveros, and Pomar families have long been associated with the structure.

A two–story Mediterranean Revival at *48 Sevilla Street* was built between 1865 and 1885. Cast stone work adds to its interesting appearance. The house originally stood on the site of the soon–to–be–built Ponce de León Hotel. A coquina well in the southeast corner of the lot could have been the Old Markland well.

The lots along Orange Street, the northern strip of today's Model Land Tract, represent the earliest tract residential housing in the quadrangle. The property was acquired in 1873 by E. F. Joyce, an artesian well contractor, who subdivided it soon after purchase. An early house believed to have been located along Orange Street is the Philander Hulett house, constructed prior to 1885. The 1894 birds–eye map lists a house in the vicinity as American House Hotel. The

Philander Hulett House was moved to *16 Mulvey Street* in order to clear a lot for construction of the Ketterlinus School. In addition to lovely Victorian residences on Orange Street, there is the former Speissegger Drug Store, now a tourist attraction. Mr. Speissegger established his store at *31 Orange Street*, on the corner of Orange and Cordova streets, in 1887.

Land Acquisition for the Model Land Tract

Publicly Mr. Flagler denied any interest in exploiting the land he was acquiring. He and his staff worked quietly. In one case, a church building was on a key piece of property. It was torn down and a new church rose in another location for the parishioners. Some of the other key acquisitions included the Old Powder House lot, north of the Smith–Ball properties. It was 10.29 acres large and fronted for 117 feet on Cordova and 330 feet on the San Sebastian River. It had been conveyed to the U.S. Government by the Spanish Crown in 1821 and was purchased by Mr. Flagler in 1886.

The Gobert lot, above the government owned land, fronted about 400 feet on Cordova between Saragossa and Carrera streets. Charles Gobert purchased the land from Dona Isable Ridaveto in 1809. Pedro Rodriguez de Cala owned a larger lot near Gobert's property. His land was eventually bought by Dr. Anderson and, with the Gobert property, was conveyed to Mr. Flager in the 1880s.

The northernmost portion of the Model Land Tract is known as the Tolomato lands, a rectangular swatch 524 feet wide between Orange and Saragossa streets. These lands date back to 1764 when Jesse Fish, a Spanish and British period trader and land dealer, acquired them from Juan Jose Elixio de la Puente. The old Spanish cemetery, Tolomato, is located on the eastern portion of the strip. Mr. Flagler acquired the southern quarter from Dr. Anderson who had partitioned it in 1887.

The Flagler Building Era

By the end of the 1880s, Mr. Flagler owned almost the entire quadrangle, an area measuring roughly a third of a mile square. He expanded his holdings by filling in the marshes west of Riberia Street. The exceptions to the Flagler holdings were land retained by Dr. Anderson in the center of the southern strip and the property along the northern border which remained under private ownership. Mr. Flagler began to build.

Ponce de León Hotel

In public statements, Mr. Flagler said his reason for acquiring so much land was directly related to development of his luxury hotel, the Ponce de León, which opened on King Street in 1888. The hotel's

Spanish Renaissance Revival appearance was the result of the combined efforts of designer Bernard Maybeck and Mr. Flagler's architects, John M. Carreré and Thomas Hastings, described in Chapter 7. The interior was carefully planned by Louis Tiffany who soon after achieved world–wide recognition for his ex-

Ponce de León Hotel, ca. 1889

cellent stained glass masterpieces. Murals were painted by George W. Maynard and angelic canvases by Virgilio Tojetti were stretched across the ceilings.

Construction of the palatial hotel was supervised by St. Augustine contractors James A. McGuire and Joseph A. McDonald who used the recently invented poured concrete technique. Developed by Franklin W. Smith, the building innovation was first used on his St. Augustine home, Zorayda Castle. Mr. Smith and Zorayda Castle are more fully described in Chapter 7. The hotel was the first major structure in the United States to be built using this method. Mr. Flagler was so pleased with the poured concrete construction method that it was used for many of his later buildings.

Grace Memorial Methodist Church

While building the grand hotel, the same team of architects and builders also worked on the Spanish Renaissance Revival Grace Memorial Methodist Church at *Eight Carrera Street*. The church harmoniously blends a Spanish motif with modern architectural styles and construction techniques. The salmon colored surfaces of the cast terra cotta decorations are in striking contrast to the rough surfaces of exposed concrete with shell aggregate. Grace Church was built at Mr. Flagler's request for the Methodist congregation who, in turn, relinquished land then occupied by Olivet Methodist Church. The little wooden church building originally stood on the site of the planned Alcazar Hotel, another Flagler inspiration translated into a building by the Carreré–Hastings team.

Memorial Presbyterian Church and Manse

By 1890 the magnificent Memorial Presbyterian Church and accompanying manse, now the church house, were in place. The church, a memorial to Mr. Flagler's daughter, Jennie Louise Benedict, was designed in the Venetian Renaissance style and was patterned after St. Mark's Cathedral in Venice. The copper dome reaches approximately 150 feet into the air. Elaborate capitols of old–gold and white terra cotta ornament the base of the dome. The three Venetian arches over the entrance are supported by red terra cotta Ionic pillars.

The the building at *36 Sevilla Street* was the home for Reverend John MacGonigle, the minister at that time. It continues the Venetian Renaissance theme. Red, white, and old–gold terra cotta ornamentation accents arched windows and doors with design elements sympathetic to those found on the church. Both buildings used the poured concrete method. Around 1925 the manse was remodeled with the addition of a spacious auditorium. The building now serves as a center of fellowship activities and community programs.

Ancient City Baptist Church

The brown–brick Ancient City Baptist Church at *27 Sevilla Street* was constructed in 1895. The Romanesque Revival church displays a cone–shaped turret above the three–story tower. Decorative brickwork ornaments the arched windows and entryway. Mr. Flagler assisted in the construction of the building by offering the lot to the then eight–year–old congregation which was in need of a church home.

Other Model Land Tract Homes and Buildings

Throughout the Model Land Tract one sees the impact of Mr. Flagler's vision. The magnificent architecture of his hotels and churches delight the eye. Lavish residences maintain their character. One of the more interesting features of the area is its variety of architectural styles. A Neo–Classical Revival style building was added to the list when Fred A. Hendrich designed the one–story school at *47 Orange Street*. St. Augustine's largest residential structure, located at *16 Riberia Street*, was built of coquina concrete block.

Mr. Flagler's pattern was to build magnificent homes for his key executives. In many cases, Mr. Flagler retained ownership of the home. A stately Colonial Revival home was built in 1894 for James E. Ingraham, an official in the Flagler enterprises. This house is located at *32 Sevilla Street* on a lot adjacent to the church properties. Mr. Ingraham served as vice president of the Florida East Coast Railway and president of the Model Land Company. He was an active community citizen serving as mayor from 1915–1920 and was one of the people active in exploring the Florida Everglades. His two–and–a–half story home was erected on a poured concrete base. The classical round wood columns, spindle work, and fanlight window are a few of the elements contributing to its style and beauty. Mr. Ingraham occupied the house until his death in 1924. At that time the property reverted to Louise Wise Lewis.

Mrs. Lewis was one of the Flagler heirs and had been the beneficiary of the estate of her aunt, Mary Lily Flagler, his third wife. Mrs. Lewis gave the elegant structure to the Presbyterian Church for use as a manse, a home for the ministers of the church. With the blessings of her children, Lawrence Lewis and Molly Lewis Wiley, the building was renovated to serve as offices and classrooms for the church. It was formally dedicated as the Mary Lily Flagler Manse during the 1990 celebration of the centennial of the church. The "Manse" name was retained in honor of Louise Wise Lewis' wishes, although it no longer serves as a residence for the pastors.

The Spades House is located at 33 *Sevilla Street*. The home was built around 1899 as a winter cottage for Michael H. Spades, a wealthy Indianapolis businessman, and was frequently the site of lavish entertainment. The large Colonial Revival house includes Ionic columns with crown mouldings and complementary flat roofs over porches and the main structure. An old photograph shows a railing surrounding the roof and decorative pilasters accenting the corners and the entrance. The current owners are renovating the 17–room house, one of the fine buildings in the Model Land Tract.

Carrera Street Houses

Another early structure in the area is a lovely Queen Anne house at 9 *Carerra Street*. Built in 1888 by McGuire and McDonald, it is one of a pair of cottages connected with the Ponce de León Hotel. The sister cottage was demolished long ago; however, Number 9 remains and shows an example of a traditional winter residence of wealthy Northerners. In the 1890s Mr. and Mrs. Alexander B. Coxe of Pennsylvania frequently rented the two–and–a–half story Victorian house. The family was noted for its golfing and yachting activities.

Later residents of the cottage included Union Captain Henry Marcotte and his wife Anna. Captain Marcotte was the leader of a chapter of the Grand Army of the Republic and author of a daily column for the *Jacksonville Florida Times–Union*, covering news about St. Augustine. Mrs. Marcotte was editor and proprietor of the entertaining gossip newspaper, *Tatler*. From 1927 to 1940 the cottage was occupied by three educators: Evelyn Hamblen, Leone Roode, and Alice B. Carrier. The building now serves as the art department and art gallery of Flagler College. It was moved a few yards forward on the site during reorganization of the Flagler campus when a new dormitory was built southwest of the old home.

A few other early homes also were residences of Flagler employees, the larger homes belonging to higher officials in his companies. The two–story house at *50 Carrera Street* was a gift from Mr. Flagler to W. L. Crawford, the superintendent of the Jacksonville, St. Augustine, and Indian River Railroad. Its current residents plan to restore the exterior and interior to its former appearance. Another early house is located at *52 Carrera Street*. Now an apartment building, it was known as the La Posada Hotel when it was built between 1885 and 1894 and stayed a hotel until the 1930s. Other early homes on Carrera Street include the one–and–a–half story homes on the western end at *67 and 71 Carrera Street*. The homes were built between 1885 and 1894 by McGuire and McDonald to house employees of the Flagler enterprises. The site of the third house, *75 Carrera Street*, is now occupied by a bank.

Casa Amarylla

One of St. Augustine's striking Colonial Revival style residences is located at *6 Valencia Street*. The two–and–a–half story wood frame building was constructed in 1898. It originally had a one–story open porch on the south side with a turned spindle balustrade and

round wood columns. An early description of the house notes the broad verandas on the south and east sides. Each room contained a fireplace with an antique mantel. A playroom was on the third floor. The first resident, Dr. Fremont–Smith, lived in the house for only one winter season. *Casa Amarylla, now Wise Hall, Flagler College*

He was a prominent physician who maintained a practice in Bar Harbor, Maine, as well as in Florida. He was a well respected hotel physician for Mr. Flagler's enterprises. By 1899 many of the wealthiest winter travelers moved south to Mr. Flagler's new resort and residential area—Palm Beach. Dr. Fremont–Smith was asked to follow and the elegant house was rented to other seasonal visitors.

One of the first renters was Charlton Yarnall, his wife and two children. Mr. Yarnall, a prominent Philadelphia financier, headed a chemical importing company and held important positions in insurance and savings corporations. Mrs. Yarnall's father was Alexander Brinton Coxe, an owner and operator of anthracite coal mines in Drifton, Pennsylvania. Mr. Coxe rented a nearby cottage.

In two separate transactions in 1899 and 1900, Henry Flagler sold the property and house to Albert Lewis who occupied the residence for more than 20 years. Mr. Lewis was known as the Pennsylvania Lumber King and lived in Bear Creek near Wilkes–Barre during the summer months. The Lewis' three children grew up in the winter cottage called "Casa Amarylla." The children were playmates of the Anderson children and General Schofield's daughter, Georgina, all of whom attended school together at *20 Valencia Street*, in the Schofield House which will be described shortly.

Mr. Lewis was a charitable and public spirited man. In addition to landscaping, the Lewis family made a number of improvements on the Valencia Street property. A two–story addition rose on the north side of the house. A coquina chimney and fireplace

Schofield House, now Offices, Flagler College

were erected on the west side, creating a congenial atmosphere in the reception hall. Always progressive, he developed an electrical plant which operated from a small coquina house on the grounds. The beautifully furnished home was considered one of the loveliest in St. Augustine. Although the family periodically used the house after Mr. Lewis' death in the 1920s, it stood empty throughout most of the 1930s.

In 1936 St. Augustinians were informed that the vacant building was to be remodeled for use as a charitable pre–school day care center. The plan was conceived by Louise Wise Lewis Francis who had married one of Mr. Lewis' sons. The idea was the product of many weeks of work she had done in a government operated nursery school in Baltimore, Maryland. As she arranged for trained personnel, local architect Fred A. Hollingsworth began work on the renovation. The large front porch was immediately replaced by a porte cochere with a semi–circular driveway. A two–story porch was built on the east side and interior features such as electricity, laundry and plumbing facilities, and kitchen modernization were undertaken. The plan was to care for 36 youngsters between the ages of three and five. Unfortunately, Mrs. Francis died before the project reached fruition and, since she did not endow the nursery school in her will, the building was sold.

Dr. Vernon A. Lockwood bought the home and continued remodeling the building, converting it into apartments. From 1940 to 1975 the former Lewis House was known as the Valencia Apartments. The last of several owners during the last three–and–a–half decades was Lawrence Lewis, Jr., the son of Louise Wise Lewis Francis. Mr. Lewis, past chairman of the Historical St. Augustine Preservation Board and chairman of the St. Augustine Restoration Foundation, Inc., conveyed the property to Flagler College for use as an office building. Students and college administrative staff now pass through the entrance of the large white house on Valencia Street. Although its appearance has been modified since the Flager era, the stately structure continues to maintain a prominent position overlooking the former hotel grounds, now part of the Flagler College Campus.

Schofield House

Unique in many respects, the masonry Victorian house at 20 Valencia Street is representative of St. Augustine's gilded era when homes of its type for winter residents attracted the elite of the country. Two such dignitaries who made the plush "cottage" their home were Union Generals John McAllister Schofield (1899–1906) and Martin D. Hardin (1916–1923) and their families. Both men were respected military leaders and had been highly decorated for their service during the Civil War. It is easy to see what attracted the Schofields and Hardins to the elegant residence. The building is a unique blend of then-popular architectural styles. Victorian spindle balusters and patterned brick-work in the gables and chimney are mixed with Colonial Revival style round wood columns and dentils. The ashlar–scored natural finish and red brick quoins with window–surrounds duplicated the color pattern of the Ponce de León Hotel across the street.

The link between the grand hotel and the fine residence is stronger than architectural coordination. The house was built between 1887 and 1891 for the first manager of the hotel, Osborn Dunlap Seavey. Mr. Seavey, a native of Maine, was a logical choice for the important position. He knew the responsibilities well, having worked with his father who successfully managed New England hostelries. Mr. Seavey's talents and abilities gained him a position as manager of St. Augustine's wooden luxury hotel, the San Marco. It was there he met Mr. Flagler who offered him a position during the planning stages of the building of the Ponce de León. Mr. and Mrs. Seavey selected most of the furniture for the hotel while organizing the staff for its opening on January 10, 1888. During this period, he also managed the Alcazar Hotel and directed the casino, Turkish baths, billiard rooms, tennis courts, bowling alleys, and ball park. His personal interest in sports and recreation enhanced the programs the Flagler hotels offered their guests. In 1891 Mr. Seavey brought baseball to St. Augustine. A local paper reported that professional teams from Chicago and Boston were scheduled to play on the first of March of that year. Mr. Seavey also formed one of the first African–American baseball teams in the coun-try, the Ponce de León Giants. The players were members of the hotel staff.

In 1894 Mr. Seavey resigned from the St. Augustine position and for a number of years the house, owned by Mr. Flagler and then the Model Land Company, was rented to winter visitors. Two prominent ladies occupied the cottage toward the end of the decade. They were Mrs. Robert Rhodes Stone and her daughter, Mrs. Lawrence Maxwell. Their link to St. Augustine was through Mrs. Stone who was the maternal great–aunt of authors William Rose, Laura, and Steven Vincent Benet, descendents of the Minorcan Benet family whose members had settled in the city in 1777.

The house became the property of Union General John McAllister Schofield in 1899. A West Point graduate, General Schofield served in the Union Army and had been in charge of military reconstruction in Virginia after the war. He later served as Secretary of War, Superintendent of the U.S. Military Academy at West Point, and Commanding General of the U.S. Army. It was due to his recommendation that the U.S. acquired Pearl Harbor as a naval base. The famed Schofield Barracks in Honolulu are named for him. He retired in September 1895 and returned to St. Augustine where he and his wife were feted at the Alcazar Hotel. The following year they rented the Ponce de León Cottage at *7 Carrera Street*, which has since been demolished. General Schofield's retirement years were active. He wrote his memoirs, chaired a convention in Tampa to consider the South Atlantic and Gulf States Harbor Defense and Improvement, and traveled with Mr. Flagler and Flagler associates throughout the county and state. The Schofields hosted many prominent guests including Admiral George Dewey, hero of the Battle of Manila. In 1901 the house was enlarged with the addition of a two–story brick wing on the west side of the building. General Schofield died in his Valencia Street home in 1906 when he was 74 years old. Flags on public buildings in St. Augustine were flown at half mast as a gesture of respect.

Union General Martin D. Hardin occupied the house from 1916 until his death in 1923 at the age of 85. A Brigadier General, he was a West Point graduate and descended from a long line of military leaders. After the Civil War, General Hardin commanded Fort Wayne, Detroit; Fort Porter, New York; and Fort Gratiot, Michigan. He retired in 1870 and pursued a career in law, practicing for 12 years in Chicago. In 1893, General Hardin married his second wife, Amelia McLaughlin, and made St. Augustine his home. Before occupying the Valencia Street house, the couple had lived on the corner of *St. Francis and*

Charlotte streets. The General is buried in the National Cemetery on Marine Street in St. Augustine.

Amelia Hardin remained in the Valencia Street house until her death in 1939. One of her contributions to the city was the restoration of La Leche Shrine on the Mission of Nombre de Dios grounds. A bronze plaque next to the door of the chapel says that it was "restored and furnished as a chapel by Mrs. General Hardin in memory of General Martin D. Hardin in 1925." The General had converted to Catholicism in the early days of the Civil War and was a devout member of the faith. Following the Hardins' occupancy, the house became the residence of Mrs. Rose Lawrence Pattie. For three decades, until the early 1970s, Mrs. Pattie resided in the house, renting out furnished rooms. The home is now owned by Flagler College and is used for faculty office space. In 1987, the College completed a $500,000 restoration project on the house. Every attempt was made to salvage as much original material as possible and architectural integrity was thoughtfully maintained. The interior was decorated to reflect the military history associated with the house, reminding visitors that for a total of 14 years this was the home of two Union Generals and their families. The Schofield House represents another unique segment of St. Augustine's history and is a fine example of a Flagler era "winter cottage."

Mediterranean Revival Architecture

The newly popular Mediterranean Revival homes were soon being built throughout the neighborhood. They provided a harmonious blend with the earlier Spanish Renaissance Revival style churches and hotels and a departure from the Victorian and Colonial Revival residences that had flourished from the 1880s and 1890s into the early 20th century.

The two–story Mediterranean Revival residence at *20 Cordova Street* was built between 1904 and 1910. The house was originally occupied by George A. Colee, a member of the family associated with the carriage and livery business since Mr. Colee established the St. Augustine Transfer Company in the 1880s. Of particular note are the arches on the front porches, the clay tile trim, and the flat roof with a parapet. The cast concrete columns, fan lights, tower, and pavilion add to the building's distinctive appearaance. A later occupant of the house was Verne E. Chatelaine, director of the St. Augustine Historical Survey for the Carnegie Commission in the late 1930s. During the 1950s and 1960s, the building served as Garcia's Funeral Home and the St. Augustine Association for Retarded Citizens. It now houses offices.

A Mediterranean Revival house at *24 Saragossa Street* was built between 1910 and 1914 by C. M. Milburn. During the 1920s and the early 1930s, it became the home of George W. Jackson, a local attorney and county judge.

State Senator Walter B. Fraser built a two–story residence in the Mediterranean style between 1910 and 1917 at *29 Valencia Street*. The Ionic columns on the portico are barely visible behind the shrubbery and trees. Senator Fraser is responsible for two of the city's tourist attractions: the Fountain of Youth and the Oldest Wooden School-house. The house was recently purchased by Flagler College and was razed in order to build a new college library.

The largest structure designed in the Mediterranean Revival style was the original Ketterlinus High School Building, which faced Mulvey Street off Orange Street. The building burned in 1985. It was designed by F. A. Hollingsworth of St. Augustine and constructed in 1925. The school. had been a junior high, middle school, and an elementary school. It was named for Elizabeth Warden Ketterlinus, donator of the land and daughter of William Warden.

Perhaps the most architecturally interesting commercial build-ing with a Mediterranean flair was the Y.M.C.A. at *59 Valencia Street*. Completed in 1907, the brick structure combined Victorian and Medi-terranean elements. The Mediterranean influence was seen in the clay tile roof and thick carved rafters. Victorian features included rounded pilasters accenting the entrance door and a turned–spindle balustrade around the one–story open porch. An early photograph of the Y.M.C.A. shows two wing extensions on the east and west sides which may have served as carriage passages. They were removed in 1956. By 1983, the building had been transferred to Flagler College. The college demolished the building and tennis courts were constructed on the site.

Model Land Company

Until the turn of the century, Mr. Flagler was undoubtedly the major influence in the development of this portion of the town. However, in the closing years of the century, his interests were turning toward Palm Beach. In 1896, the Model Land Company was incorporated to handle Mr. Flagler's extensive state–wide holdings. In 1903 Mr. Flagler transferred authority to the company and, with the stroke of a pen, conveyed title to about 37 acres north and west of the Ponce de León Hotel. From that date, the evolution of the quadrangle changed.

After Mr. Flagler deeded his real estate to the Model Land Company, the property became a Realtor's delight. By the 1916–1920 period about sixteen lots were selling per year. The lots were considerably smaller than those sold during the 1880s and 1890s. Mr. Flagler's intention to develop a neighborhood of lavish homes to complement his luxury hotel faded as economic and social situations changed. More modest houses were built, although the area surrounding the Ponce de León Hotel continued to contain the greatest percentage of elegant homes. The growing trend toward providing housing for Flagler employees, coupled with the desire to live near the Florida East Coast Railway offices and shops, created a pressing need for more lots in the western portion of the property. Between 1904 and 1910, three one–block streets were cut through: *Lemon, Almeria, and Oviedo.* The primarily one– to one–and–a–half story residences on *Lemon and Almeria streets* were frequently built in a bungalow style. Some made interesting use of the native coquina rock, using locally produced concrete block for porches and foundations and adding unique touches with cast concrete posts. The *Oviedo Street* houses were larger, reaching a peak of construction during the late teens and the early 20s.

The homes at *25 and 27 Riberia Street* are distinctive. Both are set back from the street, an indication of early Model Land Tract construction. The two–and–a–half story house at *25 Riberia Street* displays attractive Victorian features as well as a distinctive two–story bay. Number *27 Riberia Street*, with its Colonial Revival columns, and its Victorian neighbor on the left, were built between 1885 and 1894 for Flagler officials.

The elaborate Queen Anne at *28 Saragossa Street* was built for H. J. Ritchie, who sketched the 1894 birds–eye view of the city.

First Methodist Church at *120 King Street* was constructed around 1911 with a brick and stucco finish. Its design includes a castellated parapet encircling the flat roof and tower, Gothic arches and windows, and decorative brickwork and pilasters. Several buildings adjacent to the church property have been absorbed into the church complex. In 1916, the house at *77 Riberia Street* became a community center for indigent girls. It was a gift of Mary Neil Darrow, given in memory of her father, William Alan Neil. It was presented to King's Daughters, a humanitarian organization, which owned the property until 1973. From 1924 until it was sold, the County Welfare Federation was located in the former house. The building is now the church's youth center.

Many large structures on King Street have been converted into commercial buildings or boarding houses. An early 20th–century frame residence at *124 King Street* served as headquarters for the Business and Professional Women's Forum and now houses the St. Augustine Court No. 23 of the Catholic Daughters of America. The two–story residence at *136 King Street* was constructed in the early teens for the Pellicer family. Mr. X. L. Pellicer, a retired bank official, was known for his community activities, particularly those relating to the historic heritage of the city. He was the co–donor of a statue in the Cathedral courtyard which commemorates the Minorcan immigrants, a group from which his family descended. The King Street house has retained the original wood exterior and is once again a private residence after having served as an apartment house for a number of years. A later Mediterranean Revival residence on the outskirts of the Model Land Tract is located at *146 King Street* and was built shortly before 1930. The first floor housed commercial operations over the years, while the second floor served as a residence.

The four-story Florida East Coast Railway office building on the western end of King Street at *1 Malaga Street* overwhelms the smaller structures nearby. The complex of commercial style office buildings was constructed around 1924. The buildings are connected by a one–story walkway with a flat parapet roof. Decorative brick and tile work accents are attractive touches on the large structure. Beside the offices is the small Railroad Park, once the center of the Florida East Coast Railway yard.

Four other transitional period structures exist: the *St. Augustine Record* building at *154 Cordova Street*, the Odd Fellows Hall at *97 Washington Street*, the Orange Street School at *47 Orange Street*, and the Solla–Carcaba Cigar Factory at *88 Riberia Street*.

Although the basic character of the Model Land quadrangle has not changed in recent decades, some structural alterations have been made on the original buildings. Large residences are frequently converted into apartment buildings or institutional headquarters. Sometime after 1956, a frame structure was razed above a masonry first floor to create the present appearance of *30 Cordova Street*. The frame portion could have been moved from a site a few yards east where a similar one–and–a–half story structure is shown on Sanborn Fire Insurance Maps through 1914. A photograph of the house at *18 Cordova Street* shows the house in 1930 as a structure with a railing crowning the octagonal projection. The exterior is now stucco and the roof on the octagonal wing is flat.

First Christian Church at *19 Riberia Street* was remodeled from one of three buildings used by contractors McGuire and McDonald in the early 1900s. The same buildings were later used by the Florida East Coast Railway and Hotel Company Carpenter Shop. The two smaller sheds of the trio were eventually razed and the main structure converted to a church for the Seventh Day Adventist congregation before it became a house of worship for the present church group. The most recent major change can be seen from U.S. Highway 1. The Herbie Wiles Insurance complex consists of two older residences, joined by a ten–foot extension. Number *78 Saragossa Street,* a turn–of–the century house owned in the early 1900s by contractor William Fishwick, was moved eastward toward its neighbor at *76 Saragossa Street*. The two residences were linked in September of 1980 with the lot on which *78 Saragossa Street* stood now serving as a parking lot.

The Flagler era provided St. Augustine with a strong second wave of major architectural styles. It also served to refocus the town inland from the waterfront. In the next chapter, we continue inland to explore West Augustine.

First Methodist Church
Architect's Rendering, 1910

Chapter 6.
West Augustine

First Spanish Period, 1565-1763

British Decades, 1763-1784

Second Spanish Period, 1784–1821

Territorial Era, 1821-1845

Early Statehood, 1845-1888
Flagler's Golden Era, 1888-1914

Twentieth Century, 1914-present

Once called New Augustine, the neighborhood west of US Highway One remains somewhat isolated from the Ancient City. It is, however, an important part of the city's history and contains several significant structures.The western appendage of the city, known as West Augustine, was formally incorporated into St. Augustine proper in 1922.

Colonial Ownership

During the British Period, the area was part of the property owned by Anglican minister John Forbes who received it as one of the British land grants. It extended from what is now the Ravenswood area south beyond Oyster Creek, the general vicinity of Lewis Boulevard. After the Spanish regained control, the land that is now West Augustine was divided into four grants. The largest was a 1,000-acre grant conveyed to Minorcan brothers, Francisco and Juan Triay. The other three tracts, all south of Oyster Creek, were derived from the Solana, Herandez, and Huertes Grants.

Dancy Tract

The land commonly called the Dancy Tract was received by the Triay brothers in 1785. They successfully cultivated their land, supporting themselves, four other relatives, and 15 slaves. The brothers received official recognition of their claim in 1894 and traded the land four years later for property at Governor's Grant, nine miles north of St. Augustine. The Triay brothers made the land trade with Jose Peso de Burgo, a native of Corsica also a New Smyrna colony immigrant.

Sr. Peso de Burgo became a prosperous merchant and was the owner of a half interest in a commercial sailing sloop. By the time of his death in 1819, he owned four houses, an orange grove, and several plantations. His possessions ranked him as one of the wealthiest men in St. Augustine. His widow, Maria Mabrity de Burgo, sold the land, now known as Ferry Tract, to Proper Vaille and Francisco J. Avice in 1882. The transaction included all buildings and improvements on the property. The new owners apparently encountered some obstacles in their business relationship and an arbitration board declared they should dissolve the partnership. When that happened, the land was sold in 1826. After a series of transactions, it was reacquired by Mr. Avice. He cultivated the land for seven years before selling it to Colonel Francis Littlebury Dancy. Colonel Dancy was a North Carolina native, a West Point graduate, and the mayor from 1838 to 1840. His wife was Florida Forsyth Reid, the daughter of Judge Robert Raymond Reid, chief justice of the Georgia Supreme Court and territorial governor of Florida from 1839 to 1841. After 1837 the 1,000 acre tract changed names again and became known as the Dancy Tract.

Ravenswood

Of all the subdivisions included in the Dancy Tract, Ravenswood is by far the largest. The story of the area begins in 1850 when James R. Harham bought 374 acres of the Dancy property. The acreage was subsequently sold to Ann D. Greeno who held the land for five years. Her husband, George , was a grocer and liquor dealer who served as mayor from 1879 to 1882. The Greeno Tract included a small section south of the present location of King Street and west of Broadwell

Subdivision. It extended north to an area just below the current city limit. In 1870, the Greeno Tract, along with a large parcel to the north, was sold to John F. Whitney, a relative of Eli Whitney, inventor of the cotton gin. At the time of Mr. Whitney's purchase, minor signs of progress were already visible in West Augustine. For several years preceding the Civil War, stage coaches traveled the rough terrain between the St. Johns River and St. Augustine. Mule-drawn freight cars rolled across 14-1/2 miles of wooden track from Tocoi on the St. Johns River to the San Sebastian River. Some early boarding houses and hotels dotted the major thoroughfare, now King Street, to accommodate passengers on the stage coaches and the mule-powered St. Johns Railway. By 1860, iron rails and a cumbersome, steam-powered, locomotive replaced the mule train. The train and the bridge across the San Sebastian River were destroyed during the Civil War.

Although West Augustine was mostly scrub oak and pine in the 1860s, one hardy family, the Southwicks, built a home on the south side of King Street. A second pioneer, James Hartshorn, built a house in 1862 about 75 feet off King Street just west of Lewis Avenue. His farmland stretched from Hartshorn to Leonardi streets and back to the railroad tracks. Although the Southwicks and Hartshorns were the only settlers, there was a great deal of activity in West Augustine during these years. Union soldiers maintained a cow pen on the corner of the present King and Leonardi streets. A salt works operated from a bluff between River Road and Marion Street. On Wednesdays Union Soldiers brought rations from St. Augustine for county residents who traveled to West Augustine to claim their supplies.

Following the Civil War years, travel across the county was resumed. Stage coaches were frequently forced to take a circuitous route to enter St. Augustine from the north. A ferry, or more accurately a rowboat, was pressed into service to transport passengers across the San Sebastian River. For two years, Fritchieff Monson was in charge of the service, after which time Mr. Hartshorn accommodated the travelers. Mr. Hartshorn's scow, although bigger than a rowboat, was only able to transport coaches at high tide, and even then it was a risky business. By 1876, Alexander Weidman opened the first store, a one-story frame building on the northwest corner of King and Leonardi streets. Within a year Mr. Hartshorn also opened a grocery store and quickly followed with a bakery.

In the summer of 1879, a group of area land owners gathered to discuss naming the still undeveloped area. Suggestions ranged from "Arenta" and "Augusta" to Mr. Whitney's choice of "Raven's Wood." Finally, "New Augustine" was recommended and, for a while, the little settlement carried that name. Mr. Whitney's choice of a name ultimately prevailed. He also left his mark on the Ancient City with the establishment of the *St. Augustine Press*, a local newspaper with nation-wide subscribers. Although a committed St. Augustine resident, Mr. Whitney never lost his love of the north. In 1874 he subdivided his property, selling lots with the stipulation that the purchasers be northerners. He also required that purchasers agree to build and occupy a house on the lot, rather than hold their real estate for speculation. The lots cost $65. Unfortunately, Mr. Whitney's Ravenswood did not develop as rapidly as he had anticipated. However, many of West Augustine's Victorian residences are located in the Ravenswood area, particularly on Spring Street and Masters Drive .

Clark / Worley House

Clark/Worley House is one of West Augustine's oldest and most significant residences and is shown on the back cover. It is located at *212 West King Street*, almost hidden behind a supermarket seemingly lost behind 20th century progress. The pyramid tower is all that projects above the market.

The home was built in 1882 for Francis Melvin Clark, a St. Augustine railroad pioneer. Mr. Clark was associated with the St. Johns Railroad for eight years and was with the Florida East Coast Railroad for 36 years. It is said that the original structure resembled the Clark family home in New Jersey. When built, the two-story Victorian structure had no tower. During the period that Mr. Clark lived in West Augustine, he also purchased property south of the house later known as Wildwood Park. Significant changes occurred in the appearance of the frame building after 1904. New owners, Doctor Samuel Gaines Worley and his son, Samuel Moore Worley, remodeled the house to the then popular Queen Anne style. In addition to adding the three-story tower, they built a one-story bay on the front and modified the porches. Some of the original gingerbread decoration is still visible on the second-floor porch on the western facade. The Worleys established the Worley Sanatorium in 1914 which operated on the property to the east until 1923. For a time thereafter the Sanatorium building was used as a hotel, but was razed in the 1940s. Although the Clark-Worley House has been used as an apartment building for a number of years, it remains one of about a dozen Queen-Anne style buildings surviving in St. Augustine.

Barbour House

The Barbour House at *8 Arenta Street* is a fine example of Second Empire architecture, now rare in St. Augustine. The style, identified by the double-pitched Mansard roof, was popular in St. Augustine after the Civil War. Most of the Second Empire buildings of this period have been demolished over the years. The distinctive roof of the Barbour house is the last Mansard original. It was built between 1885 and 1894, probably closer to the earlier date. Reverend Charles C. McLean, of Olivet Methodist Church and its successor Grace Methodist Church, purchased the property on which the house is located in 1887 and bought the adjacent lot in 1889. Reverend McLean, who maintained leadership of the Methodist group and served as the first pastor of the new Grace Methodist Church on Carrera Street, lived in the parsonage during his tenure as minister, never occupying the West Augustine house. He maintained ownership of it, however, until 1925.

In its early days, the house was a duplex with a division through the center. The dormers of the

Barbour House, built 1885-94

Mansard roof created the third floor living space in the two-and-a-half story house. A two-story rear section shows on a 1904 Sanborn Fire Insurance Map. A one-story, wrap-around porch is also shown, as well as a one-story out building for each side of the duplex. Although directory information is sketchy for the early years, the 1904 listing shows a Mrs. Iris C. Ryder, a teacher of elocution and music, as the occupant. The 1907-08 directory lists Miss Olive Sowell as a resident. After 1917 no division line appears on maps, indicating that the house was converted to a single family dwelling by that time.

In 1925, Reverend McLean, then residing in Los Angeles, sold the house to Mrs. Julia Barbour for $2,500. The Barbour family had previously rented the house and lived in it for almost 50 years, with the last Barbour family member dying in 1973. The unusual family and the once glorious Second Empire house are the subject of a Gothic novel, *The House,* written by the current owner, June Moore Ferrell. Mrs. Ferrell and her husband, A. E. Ferrell, purchased the house in 1975 and have since worked to restore it. The much improved garden now features brick walkways, a pool, and an arching bridge. Decorative elements of the rare Second Empire building included the turned porch balustrade, pressed metal shingle roof , and applied wood trim on the gabled dormers. A balcony was added around 1988.The home stands as a fine example of St. Augustine's important architecture. The Barbour and Clark/Worley Houses add elegance to the West Augustine area. They are two of several houses of architectural and historic significance in an often overlooked part of the city.

A Victorian Home at
80 Spring Street

The house at *52 Spring Street* was built between 1890 and 1895. The two-story frame residence displays many Victorian elements including turned spindle posts, jigsawn brackets and bargeboards, and a decorative balustrade and porch frieze. One of the oldest houses in the subdivision is located at *80 Spring Street*. The interesting two-story house dominates a spacious corner lot. Jigsawn brackets and balustrades decorate the two-story open porches that project from the east side of the main structure and from the southern wing. Within Ravenswood there are also a number of more recently developed areas. A large concentration of older homes is on Chapin Avenue where several homes built between 1910 and 1930 are located.

The former Greeno Tract contains six houses on *Evergreen Street* built between 1878 and 1930. Of the nine pre-1930s subdivisions in Ravenswood, only Jackson Park, Hudwell Replat, and Fulger contain pre-1930s structures. Moving south in the Dancy Tract acreage, early development also happened just below King Street, then called Tomoka Road. A two-story wood frame building located at *8-10 Madison Street* served as the New Augustine School from about 1905 to 1925. For years, Madison Street maintained the name School Street as a descriptive reference to the building's original function. In 1925, the Evelyn Hamblen School was built at *16 Isobel Street*, serving West Augustine's elementary school children through 1990.

Wildwood Park

Emily and Lyman Southwick, from Virginia, built a two-room log house on property approximately 100 feet south of *Daniels Street* at *23 West Avenue* (now US Highway One). The small house with a gabled roof and coquina fireplace was probably built shortly after the property was purchased in 1851. Mr. Southwick was killed during the Civil War. His widow maintained the property until 1871. When she sold the land then known as Arenta, or Wildwood Park, to Manning Daniels. Mr. Daniels, a New Jersey resident, developed a magnificent grove of fruit-bearing trees including Japanese plums, persimmons, figs, pomegranates, and other exotic fruit. He was not satisfied with a two-room log house and immediately built a three-story mansion with a broad veranda and a yard that was a horticulturist's dream. Whispers of Spanish days gone by echoed along the eastern border of Wildwood Park where the remains of a Spanish redoubt, still surrounded by a moat, survived the changing times.

Wildwood Park, a portion of which was called the Daniels Subdivision, was not developed for residential use until after the Wildwood Park Development Company acquired the land around 1905. The company began selling the subdivided lots around 1911 with construction occurring in 1917 and later. With the subsequent construction of U.S. Highway One came the influx of commercial structures and the displacement of residences. The area remains a mixed commercial and residential neighborhood today.

The final portion of the Dancy Tract was sold in 1869 and contains the subdivisions known as Bravo Park, Leonardy, and Broadwell. The land was purchased from Colonel Dancy by Cipriana Bravo, the wife of Cristobal Bravo and Eulogia Rogero, the wife of A. D. Rogero. The land lay west of the Southwick property and extended south from Tomoka Road to Oyster Creek.

The Bravo's portion of the mutually owned land consisted of four acres at the eastern margin of the tract, bordering on Daniels' property. Cristobal Bravo had been born in St. Augustine, the son of a Spanish Army officer. He saw military action while serving in the Florida Militia during the Second Seminole War. When the Union Army approached St. Augustine in 1862, Cristobal Bravo, then acting mayor, was forced to surrender the city to the federal officers. The Bravo family cultivated their West Augustine property developing an orange grove and growing guava, fig, and other fruit trees. After Mr. Bravo's death in 1886, Dr. Franklin Marsh, a local physician, acquired the property. He subdivided the land for residential development and named the area Bravo Park. Although sales date from 1888, only three pre-1930 structures remain. All are on West King Street and all were built in 1917.

Solana Tract

The three smaller land grants in West Augustine lie south of Oyster Creek. The earliest of these was a 100-acre grant given to Felipe Solana in 1791 by Governor Juan Quesada. Mr. Solana cultivated the land, a southeasterly parcel, residing there with his family of eight and his 11 slaves. After Mr. Solana's death in 1821, the land was conveyed to his heir, Bartolo de Castro. It eventually became part of the Seminole Park Subdivision, a post-1930 development.

Hernandez Tract

The second of the three small grants was a twenty-acre plot received by Martin Hernandez in 1798. His land was northwest of the Solana Tract and below the larger Huertes Grant. It extended west from the San Sebastian River to what is today the South Dixie Highway and south from River Road to a line below, but parallel with, State Road 207. Mr. Hernandez, a native of Minorca, was chief carpenter of the royal works of fortifications. His son, Jose Mariano Hernandez, was a noted military officer during the 1830s Seminole Indian Wars and was a prominent citizen during the Territorial Period. In addition to the West Augustine grant, Mr. Hernandez owned El Naranjal, the Spanish grant which eventually became Atwood Tract subdivision in the southwestern peninsula of St. Augustine. The Spanish ferry landing was located at the Hernandez Grant, opposite Kings Ferry Road which formed the southern boundary of El Naranjal.

Mr. Hernandez cultivated his 20-acres and built three structures on the land prior to the American occupation in 1821. The grant was subdivided in the 1920s forming Hernandez or Andalucia Park Subdivision. Eighteen pre-1930s residences remain standing in the subdivision divided by U.S. Highway One.

Huertas Tract

In 1813 Antonio Huertas received 800 acres of land from Governor Sebastian Kindelan. The property borders Oyster Creek and the

San Sebastian River and extends along River Road to South Dixie Highway which it follows south to just below Florida State Road 207. Records show that Sr. Huertas lived on Bridge Street and was a Protestant. However, no documents show how he used his land. In 1822 James Forbes, the son of the original owner, reacquired this section of the family estate. Mr. Forbes, an early territorial mayor of St. Augustine and U.S. Marshal of Florida, sold the land to the local Catholic priest, Rev. Benedict Medeore, in 1856. It remained in the hands of Catholic officials until 1880 when it was subdivided and sold.

Major William Aiken of Kentucky purchased a large plot and in 1883 built his mansion, Vista del Rio. He raised crops and rare plants on the 13-acre estate. The house still stands at *24 Anderson Street*, although it has been altered over the years. The wooden siding of the two-and-a-half story Victorian residence has been stuccoed over and the original two-story open porch as been replaced by a small entry portico. Pierced and jigsawn rafters are still visible on the stately structure. The beautiful home on the banks of the San Sebastian River was often praised in local newspapers. After Major Aiken's death, the property was used for a time by the American Silk Producing and Manufacturing Company. The house was later owned by two prominent St. Augustinians: Brigadier General Clifford R. Foster, adjutant general of Florida, who owned the property from 1924 to 1926, and Senator Verle Pope.

A large plot of land has remained in the hands of the Davis family and its extensions since the turn of the century. The two-story wood frame house at *41 South Whitney Street* was built in the 1890s and was the residence of Lawrence O. Davis, a county commissioner for almost two decades. His son, L. O. Davis, served as County Sheriff for 21 years.

From time to time within the earlier chapters we have emphasized the work of the engineers and architects who worked to build St. Augustine. In the next section, some of the city's remarkable architectural styles are discussed, as are a number of architects, and buildings which have been lost.

Chapter 7.
Architecture in Focus

Although the work of a number of architects has been emphasized at various points throughout the text, in this section additional architects, styles of architecture, and lost architecture are emphasized beginning with the 19th century architects.

Robert Mills

By the 19th century, several prominent architects began to work in St. Augustine. Robert Mills (1781–1855), born in Charleston, South Carolina, is recognized as being America's first native–born architect. He studied with James Hoban, designer of the White House, and became a protege of Thomas Jefferson, for whom he served two years as a draftsman at Monticello. Mr. Mills worked for five years in the same capacity for Benjamin Latrobe. Mr. Latrobe is generally known as America's first professional architect and designer of the House Chamber and America's first city water supply system in Philadelphia. Following his work with Mr. Latrobe, Mr. Mills entered private practice. He designed the two wings added to Independence Hall in Philadelphia and the Brockenbrough House in Richmond, which later served as the White House of the Confederacy. Nationally, he is best remembered for his work on the Washington Monument in Washington, D.C.

In St. Augustine, he was considered the city's pioneer preservation architect for his design work on Government House in 1833.

The Cathedral-Basilica overlooking Government House, ca. 1951

127

According to his biographer, Mr. Mills tried "to guarantee unspoiled the harmonies achieved by its original builders...Mr. Mills was especially meticulous in the matter of tiles for this old Spanish building, particularly on the floors of the galleries, in order to preserve exact agreement in color, and to reveal no new work." His bill for "designs, drawings, plans, and estimates of alterations and improvements to the Court House at Saint Augustine" was $100. All traces of Mr. Mills' work on Government House vanished with the remodeling of the building in the 1870s and its reconstruction in the 1930s. Although no trace of his work remains, it is important to recognize the calibre of the architectural talent working for St. Augustine during the Territorial period.

Andrew Jackson Davis and James Renwick were equally important architectural figures. Their contributions to the city are emphasized elsewhere in the text.

Franklin W. Smith and the Villa Zorayda

Franklin W. Smith was a Boston hardware merchant and amateur architect. His hobby was inspired by a visit to the Crystal Palace Exposition in London in 1851 and by subsequent European travels. He began by building small–scale models. When his company became successful, and he became wealthy, he began to construct full–scale buildings. The Villa Zorayda, inspired by the Alhambra in Spain, was his first. The Villa, located at 83 King Street, was designed as his home. Although he had a classical design in mind, he used the new poured concrete construction method. Mr. Flagler was so impressed with the innovative building material that he would soon begin using the same technique in his hotels and churches.

Shortly after completing Villa Zorayda, he built the House of Pansa at Saratoga Springs, New York, where he reproduced one of the buildings in Pompeii that had been covered by the eruption of Mount Vesuvius. In 1891 he published an elaborate *Design and Prospectus for the National Gallery of History and Art at Washington, D.C.* It called for reproducing the Parthenon, the Pantheon, the Alhambra, St. Peter's Basilica, the Taj Mahal, and other famous buildings in the nation's capital. His St. Augustine friend, Mr. Renwick, provided design sketches for the prospectus Mr. Smith published in 1891.

Nine years later the Government Printing Office published his prospectus along with his equally ambitious $38 million proposal of *Designs, Plans, and Suggestions for the Aggrandizement of Washington* which called for, among other things, a new and more elaborate Executive Mansion and a National Avenue featuring homes from all the states. The grand proposals never came to pass, but they form an interesting footnote to the City Beautiful Movement that swept the country in the aftermath of the Columbian World's Fair in 1892–93. In 1897, with the financial assistance of S. Walter Woodward, he built the "Halls of the Ancients" on New York Avenue in Washington, D.C., using Roman, Egyptian, Assyrian, and Saracenic architecture.

John M. Carreré and Thomas Hastings

Carreré and Hastings was one of the country's leading architectural firms in the late 19th century and early 20th century. Both men had studied at the Ecole des Beaux Arts in Paris and then worked together in the New York office of McKim, Mead, and White.

In 1885, Mr. Flagler commissioned them to design the Ponce de León Hotel. With that commission, they founded their own firm and pioneered the Spanish Renaissance Revival style prevalent in the hotel, the neighboring Alcazar Hotel, and the nearby Grace Methodist Church. "Before drawing the plans for these structures," Mr. Hastings recalled later, "I spent much time roaming around St. Augustine endeavoring to absorb as much of the local atmosphere as possible. I wanted to retain the Spanish character of St. Augustine and so designed the buildings in keeping with the architecture of the early houses here with their quaint overhanging balconies."

The Venetian Renaissance style Memorial Presbyterian Church and the adjacent church house were also designed by Carreré and Hastings. In the Model Land Tract, they designed the Flagler residence, Kirkside, a magnificent Georgian Colonial Revival estate as well as a number of elegant residences. Kirkside is described in more detail in chapter 8. Messrs. Carreré and Hastings left St. Augustine with their firm's reputation firmly established. Their later work reflected French rather than Spanish Renaissance themes and included the New York Public Library, the Senate and House Office Buildings in Washington, D.C. , and the opulent Flagler mansion, Whitehall, in Palm Beach.

Mr. Carreré was killed in an automobile accident in 1911. After his death, Thomas Hastings continued to design notable structures, including the Frick Museum in New York.

St. Augustine's Resident Architects

Professional schools of architecture were mainly a post–Civil War phenomenon in America. For this reason, many early practitioners were builders or engineers. They designed houses and business structures "on the side." The 1885-1886 St. Augustine city directories listed Sigmund von Gemmiger as an "architect and civil engineer." Heth Canfield was an "architect, carpenter, builder, building mover, and manufacturer of window or door screens." Mr. Canfield later served as president of the St. Augustine Improvement Company which built many Victorian homes in the southwest section of town. S. Bangs Mance, in an advertisement in 1885, listed himself as an "architect and builder of the Magnolia Hotel." The original portion of the Magnolia was an 1840s structure; however, Mr. Mance was responsible for the more familiar Victorian addition. He later built the Lyon Building and houses at *11 and 15 Bridge Street.* Gould T. Butler, a later practitioner in the same vein, advertised himself as "civil engineer and architect." He designed the Matanzas Apartments on the Bayfront and the Alf B. Day House on Anastasia Island. Mr. Butler also prepared the 1923 official city map.

Notable among 20th century professional architects who lived and worked in St. Augustine were Fred A. Henderich and Francis A. Hollingsworth. Mr. Henderich was the outstanding local bungalow designer. Hallmarks of his work include natural finish wood shingles, palmetto tree porch posts, and coquina fireplaces and chimneys. He designed many homes along south St. George Street. Larger examples of his residential work can be found at *178 Avenida Menendez* and *21 Water Street*. In the 1920s he redesigned the Abbott Mansion at *14 Joiner Street* and the house at *282 St. George Street*. Mr. Henderich's later work was in the Mediterranean Revival style, often using coquina shell dash stucco as an exterior finish. He designed the old Flagler Hospital at the south end of Marine Street after the original building was destroyed by fire. In the 1930s, he was the architect for the Civic Center on San Marco Avenue, one of the last major coquina buildings constructed in St. Augustine. Mr. Hollingsworth was also noted for his Mediterranean Revival works: the original Ketterlinus School facing Mulvey Street and the First Union Bank Building, St. Augustine's only skyscraper, at *24-28 Cathedral Place*.

Moorish Revival Architecture

The mention of Moorish–style architecture frequently conjures up visions of castles with massive walls and towers, often austere, bleak structures. Images of onion-shaped domes and intricate geometric designs also come to mind. No onion-shaped domes exist in St. Augustine; rather it is the former image that more accurately describes the buildings that are classified as Moorish Revival. A flat roof with projecting battlements is one criterion. Horseshoe-shaped arches are another. Ornamenal ironwork and geometric patterns are also elements which set the tone for the exotic style.

There are eight Moorish Revival buildings in St. Augustine. The four most visible are the Villa Zorayda, now known as Zorayda Castle, at *83 King Street*; the Castle Warden, now Ripley's Believe It or Not Museum, at *19 San Marco Avenue*; the Cordova Hotel, now the St. Johns County Courthouse, at *99 Cordova Street*; and the Lyon Building on the corner of *King and St. George Streets*. The other four are the commercial building at *152–156 St. George Street* and residences at *15 Shenandoah Street, 33 Old Mission Road, and 174 Avenida Menendez*.

Villa Zorayda

An early photograph of the Villa Zorayda when it was a cafe in the 1920s

Villa Zorayda, built in 1883, was the pioneer Moorish–style structure in the city. Residents watched as the walls of the unique structure rose at *83 King Street*.

Franklin Waldo Smith was architect, builder, and owner. His building procedures were of enormous interest. The castle was constructed of poured concrete, a method he developed in order to achieve design elements from buildings in the "mysterious East" without importing stone to build the massive walls.

Mr. Smith looked for a suitable building method and found his answer in Switzerland while watching workmen construct concrete partition walls by casting them from the left–over building material of the main walls. From this he determined that a mixture of coquina shell and newly discovered Portland cement would create substantial stone walls worthy of his design. The venture was so successful that it was repeated again and again in walls forming the magnificent Flagler buildings constructed a few years later. Mr. Smith's exotic building won immediate acclaim. It was the first building of its kind in the

United States. The exterior of Villa Zorayda displays numerous windows of varying shapes and sizes; one is a reproduction of the exquisite latticed windows of Cairo. Recessed porches and balconies add to the exotic effect. A large two–story courtyard inside the building is surrounded on both levels by a gallery of beautiful Moorish arches supported by light, graceful columns. Tiles made in Spain adorn the courtyard and walls. The arches are decorated with Arabic relief work. The effect is a refined interpretation of the beauty of the Alhambra. Alhambra Palace in Spain was his inspiration. The Villa was named for one of the beautiful princesses in Washington Irving's *Tales of the Alhambra*.

Mr. and Mrs. Smith and their daughter Nina participated in social events during the winter seasons in St. Augustine. Nina published a book titled *Tales of St. Augustine* in 1891 when she was 17 years old. The work was reprinted in 1903 as *Among the Palms*. In 1898, the Smiths decided to sell the house; however, there were no immediate buyers and in 1900 the building was opened to the public as a tourist attraction. Finally, in 1903, the Villa, along with the neighboring Granada Hotel, were leased to Ira C. Rinehart. The terms of the lease included all the furnishings in both buildings. Mr. Rinehart was listed in the 1904 directory as proprietor of the Villa, but by 1907 Budd Long is mentioned, this time as proprietor of the Zorayda Club. In the ensuing years the Villa functioned as a club, restaurant, gambling casino, hotel, private residence, and tourist attraction.

Sometime after Mr. Smith's death in 1911, the Villa was acquired by Abraham S. Mussallem, a native of Lebanon who came to St. Augustine during the Flagler era. Mr. Mussallem, a dealer in antiques and Oriental rugs, added interesting items to the residence, including a set of inlaid chairs and tables. The furniture was a gift to him from the Egyptian government in gratitude for his work on the Egyptian display at the Chicago World's Fair in 1933. Mr. Mussallem occupied the Villa for several years before his death in 1941. The Villa served as a residence for the Mussallem family and, under their direction, also functioned as a tourist attraction during the mid–1930s. The building was closed to visitors during the Second World War. Mrs. Olga Mussalem operated the Castle from the late 1940s until her death in 1954. In 1964 it was reopened by members of the family as Zorayda Castle.

Casa Monica

In 1886, soon after completing the Villa Zorayda, Mr. Smith began work on the Casa Monica project named for Monica, the mother of St. Augustine, Bishop of Hippo. The three– to four–story Moorish Revival hotel building at *99 Cordova Street* extends along King and Cordova streets. Again, the poured concrete method of construction was used. The building had three towers, two with battlements, the third with clay tile hip roofs. Balconets with ornamental ironwork and larger balconies with wooden turned spindle posts complement the exterior. Decorative tile and thick jigsawn rafters complete the look. The Cordova Street facade originally consisted of a three–story arcade, its graceful arches and delicately designed balustrades blending with the Moorish motif. Unable to support the venture, he sold the hotel to Henry M. Flagler in 1889, two years after its completion. Mr. Flagler changed the name to Cordova and annexed the building to his Alcazar Hotel across the street. For a time, an enclosed walkway across Cordova Street linked the two buildings.

The Cordova prospered in the 1890s with numerous small shops serving the public from the ground floor level. They included El Unico, a specialty gift shop; Asaboonian and Simonian, a curiosity shop; H. W. Davis Clothing; Smith and Woodman, druggists; and W. J. Henry, bicycles. In 1900 renovations were made modifying many of the hotel rooms into comfortable apartments. In 1932, because of the depression, the hotel closed. It was purchased in 1961 by the Florida East Coast Hotel Company which, in turn sold it to the St. Johns County Commission. The old hotel underwent extensive remodeling, including replacing the arcade with classical columns. After seven years, the building reopened as the St. Johns County Courthouse.

Lyon Building

Adjacent to the Cordova is the Moorish Revival Lyon Building built in 1886-87 and designed to conform with the neighboring hotel. Contractor S. Bangs Mance erected the structure again using the poured concrete method with an original design consisting of three-

and-a-half stories with a Mansard roof. The building included five-story, flat-roofed towers topped with battlements at the northeast and southeast corners. Balconies projected from the fourth floor. By 1899 the Mansard roof was replaced by a full fourth story. After the turn of the century balconies were added to the St. George Street side, some of which have since been removed.

Two arched doors with fanlight windows on the King Street side have been remodeled out of existence. On the St. George Street side, two doors have been filled in and covered with ceramic tile and metal grillwork. Ceramic tile has also been added to some of the window and door surrounds. Other architectural features include wooden arches with a filigree pattern above several of the windows, and jigsawn rafters below the main roof.

The impressive Lyon Building sits on a lot formerly occupied by the residence of Benjamin A. Putnam, who served as commander of the "Mosquito Roarers" of the Seminole War. He was a legislator in Territorial days and the early Statehood period, mayor, and commander of the Confederate militia known as the St. Augustine Independent Blues. Mr. Putnam, for whom the neighboring county is named, died in the late 1860s. His house was operated as Mrs. Gardner's Boarding House until it was purchased by Walter Lyon. Mr. Lyon was a Vermont native who came to Florida in 1868. His firm, Walter Lyon and Company sold groceries, hardware, crockery, furniture, and building materials from the Putnam House.

In addition to the Lyon Company's varied merchandise, Kernan's Ponce de León Pharmacy, the St. Augustine Gas and Electric Company, and the YMCA also occupied the building. Office space for doctors, dentists, and lawyers was available on the upper floors. Guleserian and Altoonjian operated a Persian Bazaar curiosity shop on the ground floor. For only 25 cents, Mme. Nino offered her talents in Palmistry in the Oriental Gypsy Camp in the building. The Lyon Company eventually went out of the retail business, but continued to manage the building. In 1908, the company advertised furnished rooms and for many years it functioned as the Lyon Hotel with stores on the ground floor.

Although a fire in 1938 burned the top floor, the neighboring Cordova Hotel escaped damage. Only water damage occurred on the lower floors of the Lyon Building. For years, owners Alfons Bernhard and John Bernworth left upper floors vacant, renting only the refurbished first floor. After the death of both partners in the late 1970s, the structure was sold, but no renovation was done except for the rented first floor stores and offices. A portion of the building facing King Street was gutted and remodeled to accommodate a fast food establishment. However, the facade was renovated in keeping with the Moorish influence. Since 1989, the St. Augustine Jaycees have used the second floor as a Halloween haunted house. This use marks the first time in over 50 years that the public was able to enter the second floor of the building.

The Lyon Building's potential is tremendous. The tile work alone suggests that preservation efforts are warranted before further deterioration of one of the city's important remaining Moorish Revival occurs.

Castle Warden

The largest Moorish Revival private residence, and the largest poured concrete private residence, was constructed in 1887 at *19 San Marco Avenue* facing the Fort Green. The building was erected for William G. Warden, one of Mr. Flagler's associates at Standard Oil. Although Mr. Warden chose not to invest in Mr. Flagler's many building projects, he did choose to become a winter resident and built the spacious Moorish castle. He was influenced by Mr. Smith's unique Villa Zorayda.

The Warden family maintained an active social schedule in St. Augustine as reported by *Tatler*. Mr. Warden was influential in the development of St. Augustine's Gas and Electric Light Company, Improvement Company, and provided financial backing for community educational needs, including the Warden Academy. Over the years, the Warden's many children married and returned with their families for winter visits. The family's interest in St. Augustine continued in several ways. William G., Jr. and Clarence, two of the sons, served for years as president and vice president of the St. Augustine

Improvement Company. Herbert Warden, another son, was vice president of the St. Augustine Golf Club to which many family members belonged. Perhaps the most generous and lasting contribution to the city came from the Warden's daughter, Elizabeth Ketterlinus who donated land to the county for a new school named in her honor.

Castle Warden was vacant for years after the senior Wardens died. In 1941, it was purchased by Norton Baskin who remodeled the building and opened it as Castle Warden Hotel. Mr. Baskin's wife was Pulitzer prize winning novelist Marjorie Kinnan Rawlings. Mr. Baskin sold the hotel in 1946. In 1948, Castle Warden was purchased by Daniel Crawford, Jr. of Philadelphia. The building was used as a hotel until 1950 when it became a museum for Ripley's Believe It or Not exhibits.

For years, the exotic "castle" dominated the view north of the city with battlements and massive chimneys rising above the four-story building. Round windows, called rose windows, were positioned along the top story just above a row of dentils. The windows and loggia have arched heads in Tuscan and Moorish patterns. Numerous alterations have occurred over the years. A loggia was added at the turn–of–the–century and a three–story wing on the east was built shortly thereafter. A fourth–story section consisting of two arched windows and two rose windows was removed in the 1940s. Some portions of the porch and loggia have been enclosed over the years. In 1987 an addition was built to include arches replicating those of the original structure. Two years later the interior was magnificently restored and exhibits were updated.

A Moorish Revival building, virtually camouflaged by awnings and commercials signs, is the two–story structure at *152–156 St. George Street*. It houses Jr. Department Store and Benjamin's Men's Shop. The building was constructed between 1885 and 1888 at the peak of the Moorish Revival fervor. Hallmarks of the style include Moorish window lines, a heavily ornamented parapet, and metal balconies similar to those on the Cordova Hotel. The building was originally owned by E. Mission, a curiosity dealer who specialized in alligator teeth, boars' tusks, sea shells, and Florida scenes for tourists. In 1902, Edward B. Genovar opened a barber shop in the building. For a time

W. A. MacWilliams maintained a law office there. Mr. MacWilliams served in both houses of the state legislature and as one of the organizers and presidents of the Florida State Bar Association.

The two remaining Moorish buildings are residences at *33 Old Mission Avenue* and *174 Avenida Menendez*. The *33 Old Mission Avenue* house was built between 1885 and 1894. It is a perfect example of "good things coming in small packages." Unlike the grand structures typical of Moorish Revival style, the little house interprets the style on a smaller scale. The flat roofs of the porch and main building have heavily decorated parapets of cast concrete Moorish ornamentation. The corners are trimmed with rusticated quoins and the porch has three Tuscan arches along the street side. The distinctive front fence is one of only two surviving Moorish–style fences in the city—the other being the fence surrounding Castle Warden.

The original owner of the Moorish cottage was Horace Walker, who occupied it for 30 years. Mr. Walker was an artesian well driller. After 1915, Mr. Walker left his Moorish house to become one of the early landowners of the Fullerwood Park subdivision. He rented his house to Florida East Coast Railway employees before selling it in 1922 to Thomas Filledes, a confectionery store proprietor.

A later example of Moorish Revival style architecture is found in the house at *174 Avenida Menendez*. Built in 1891 for brothers Charles S. and Tracy Brooks, the residence was called Brooks Villa. Although the house lacks the ornamental parapet typical of most Moorish Revival buildings, the horseshoe arches on the facade exemplify the style. Two rows of ornamental tile work adorn the front and decorative columns under the arches match those found on the Alcazar Hotel. The one–story porch on the south was a later addition, incorporated onto the house between 1910 and 1917. Beginning in the 1960s, the Moorish building was occupied by Dr. Maurice Leahy, author, lecturer, and president of the Oriel Society, an international Catholic organization. His association with the group led to the renaming of the residence, Oriel House.

Lost Architecture

For many people in St. Augustine, reviving fine old buildings is a mission. Unfortunately, too many of St. Augustine's irreplaceable treasures have been lost to decay, indifference, and progress. St. Augustine, not atypically, has had buildings go up, come down, be renovated,be relocated, and be razed.

Lost by Fire

Although the fire damage occurring during repeated raids in the Colonial Era has been emphasized, fire continued to plague St. Augustine well into the 20th century. Fire damage has taken its toll of the city's architecture with far greater frequency than any natural disaster.

The fire of 1887 swept through the Plaza area gutting the Cathedral, B. E. Carr's house on the Bayfront at 46 *Avenida Menendez*, and practically destroying the public Market Place. The four–story wooden St. Augustine Hotel on the north side of the Plaza was completed destroyed. The marketplace, however, was restored by Edward E. Vaill who owned that structure as well as the ill–fated hotel. With financial aid from Mr. Flagler, Mr. Vaill replaced the hotel with a series of commercial buildings, now known as the Vaill Block on Cathedral Place. The Carr house was rebuilt to its original appearance. However, rather than coquina, poured concrete was used as the primary building material. The building now houses the Chart House Restaurant.

The most tragic loss of the 1887 fire was the destruction of the Cathedral which had served the Catholic community since 1797. The walls that withstood the flames were used as reconstruction began on the portion of the building now south of the transept. The new transept and chancel were part of a major restoration which included building the commanding bell tower, designed by famed architect and St. Augustine winter resident, James Renwick.

Before memories of the 1887 fire diminished, a second major fire swept through town in 1895. It caused considerable damage downtown, burning the Carcaba Cigar Factory on Hypolita Street and a little Moorish Revival style residence called La Casita on the Bayfront near the Fort. Rather than try to rebuild, the cigar factory moved to the former St. Mary's Convent on St. George Street.

Two years later, St. Augustine's finest wooden luxury hotel, the San Marco, burned to the ground. The hotel had graced the city with its stately bearing and soaring seven–story towers. Although only a decade old at the time it burned, it was not replaced. At the time, Mr. Flagler's magnificent concrete structures were prospering and the cost to restore the old hotel would have been prohibitive.

The greatest destruction to the Bayfront area resulted from a fire in 1914 which roared through the heart of the city claiming four hotels, the courthouse, the Opera House, and countless homes and businesses. The Florida House Hotel at *St. George and Treasury streets*

Vedder Museum prior to burning in 1914

was where the fire started. The hotel was demolished and its Victorian towers were lost. The Monson Hotel on the Bayfront at *32 Avenida Menendez* was destroyed and later rebuilt with a new look. Beside it, on the corner of Bay and Treasury Streets, was an old coquina house that had functioned as the Vedder Museum of Natural Sciences for several years. The museum and its contents were consumed by flame. Only the base of a wall remains.

Fire struck again the next year when the Florida National Guard Headquarters at *82 Marine Street* burned leaving only the walls. There was an effort made to tear down the remains and build a modern apartment complex on the site. Fortunately, the barracks were rebuilt in keeping with the former appearance.

All was relatively quiet for a decade. Then, two days after Christmas in 1926, the wooden Magnolia Hotel on *St. George and Hypolita Streets* was reduced to ashes. The Magnolia had been built in the 1840s and extensively remodeled and enlarged in the 1880s to compete with the larger Flagler hotels. Architecturally, the most noticeable loss was the Victorian wing with its cone–shaped tower. The hotel was not replaced.

Lost by Demolition

Although these and other buildings are no longer in place, old photographs provide a means of appreciation and better understanding of a lost heritage. For example, there were three pre–Civil War mansions in the downtown area which were victims of demolitions over the years.

Cobb House, once located at the corner of *King Street and Central Avenue,* was used as a hospital during the Civil War. After the war it became the home of Abijah Gilbert, a United States Senator from Florida during the Reconstruction Era. In the 20th century the house was the frequent site for garden parties held on its spacious grounds. The house was demolished in 1950.

Also demolished was the home of General Peter Sken Smith, located next to Trinity Episcopal Church. It had been remodeled and enlarged in the 1880s when converted into the St. George Hotel. Among its patrons over the years was silent film idol Rudolph Valentino. Cited as a fire hazard, the hotel was demolished during World War II. The third grand old house was the Benjamin Putnam residence on the site of the Lyon Building.

San Marco Avenue is probably the most obvious victim of progress in the city. The attractive Victorian building at *102 San Marco,* built between 1879 and 1885, is one of the last reminders of the early period of development along the street. The Masters Homestead at *100 San Marco* was once a large rambling frame house with a tower. Today it is a memory. P. F. Carcaba, the cigar maker, had a house with towers and angles at the corner of Bridge Street.

A house replaced by a parking lot was the "stick style" Victorian Lorillard Villa on St. George and Hypolita streets. The home of rare architectural design was the winter residence of George Lorillard of the tobacco family.

Not to be forgotten are the extinct hotels that did not disappear in flames. The Barcelona Hotel evolved from the 1870s estate of Henry Ball originally located on the corner of Valencia and Sevilla Streets. The house was moved in the late 1880s to the corner lot one block north and converted into the hotel. The building became a parking lot in 1962. The Alencia Hotel, once known as the Valencia Hotel, was located on St. George near St. Francis Street. One can still walk through the wrought iron gate onto the ground where the hotel once stood. The site is now a parking lot for the St. Francis Inn at *279 St. George Street*.

Kirkside

One of the greatest architectural and historic losses is Kirkside, the Flagler estate. Mr. Flagler and his second wife, Ida Alice, built their winter residence on a lot adjacent to the Presbyterian Church he commissioned in memory of his daughter. The Georgian Colonial Revival style mansion, shown on the back cover, was designed by Carreré and Hastings. After Mrs. Flagler's illness and death, the house fell into disrepair and in the 1950s was demolished. All that remains are massive Ionic columns that had once accentuated a two–story high portico. The columns now embellish an apartment complex facing a private drive behind houses on Valencia Street.

In some instances, the city's architectural heritage is lost through alteration of the physical appearance of a building. Fine architectural details wear out in time, or having gone out of style for a period, are replaced. Delicate gingerbread patterns were stripped from Victorian porches, graceful towers were flattened, balconies were removed.

In the appendices, the city's heritage is examined through some of its interesting people and public monuments, walls, cemeteries, and other important aspects of what makes America's First City so special.

Lorillard Villa as it stood on St. George Street before demolition

Appendix 1.

Art in St. Augustine

Short–lived though it was, St. Augustine was at one time the winter artist's colony for several talented and successful artists. Many of the paintings executed by the artists of the St. Augustine colony provided the first view of Florida seen by Northerners and residents abroad. The era of easels, paints, and palettes did not blossom for almost over three centuries after the founding of St. Augustine. During that time, only a limited number of renderings were produced to provide a sketchy image of the emerging city, and little information about the artists.

Ironically, the earliest Florida sketches did not come from a member of the Menéndez crew, but from a French artist, Jacques Le Moyne. M. Le Moyne penned sketches of Fort Caroline and neighboring Indian villages while accompanying the ill–fated expedition led by French Huguenot Jean Ribault. A few maps with rough sketches survive. These include the 1588 Boazio map of the Drake attack of 1586; a 1595 sketch of the town and environs; and an illustration of the 1740 Oglethorpe raid which provides a first glance at the early settlement. Two watercolors done in 1764 show a view of Government House and a waterfront guardhouse as they appeared to the British.

It was not until the mid–1800s that a comprehensive look at the Bayfront was produced. The engraving by John S. Horton is an invaluable source of visual information about St. Augustine around 1850. Oil paintings by George Harvey also give insight of that period. Two known paintings depict the Plaza and a City Gate with the Fort in the background. In 1867 Henry J. Morton, a minister who received an apointment to St. Augustine, sketched several local scenes including the Jesse Fish estate on Anastasia Island, Government House, and Bayfront scenes.

Several other well–known artists are linked to the city in unusual ways. Eliah Vedder's (1826–1923) works included the illustrations for the Rubaiyat of Omar Khayyan. Mr. Vedder frequently came to St. Augustine to visit his father, Nicholas, who operated a museum of ancient maps and relics in a bayfront building where the Monson Motel is now located. The artist, whose popularity had soared by the early 1890s, was commissioned to paint several murals for a college arts building, a multimillionaire's house, and the Library of Congress. In 1896 he was working on the Library of Congress mural when the senior Vedder died and Elihu returned to pay his last respects to his father, and probably the city. Working in the same general time period was the English–born artist Thomas Moran (1837–1926) who established himself in New York around 1872. Mr. Moran, a follower of the Hudson River School, traveled to St. Augustine in 1877. His art work included historical subject matter, including the story of Ponce de León.

Randolph Caldecott (1846–1886) was an Englishman whose wit and grasp of human nature was manifested in illustrations, painting, and sculpture. His charming illustrations in children's books earned him the title of Lord of the Nursery. His prolific career provided much enjoyment to the world. He died on February 13, 1886 in St. Augustine and was buried in Evergreen Cemetery where his admirers still come to pay their respects.

James Calvert Smith (1879–1962) was a Florida–born artist whose successful career included a series of oil paintings known as Great Beginnings. His works now hang in the Library of Congress and other significant public spaces. As an illustrator, his work appeared in *Life, Judge, Harpers, Saturday Evening Post* and other magazines with more 14,000 illustrations printed. In the 1940s, Mr. Smith returned to St. Augustine for several winter visits. His childhood memories of 19th century St. Augustine prompted him to paint scenes of days gone by. The results included pictures of the Indians at Fort Marion, the interior of Capo's Bath House during Men's Time and Ladies' Time, and numerous landmarks. Mr. Smith's most significant contribution to the city is the 5' x 8' oil painting of the *Changing of the Flags*, an event that took place at the Castillo de San Marcos on July 10, 1821. The historic painting shows the beginning of United States rule of the area and the end of the second Spanish era. Painted according to a description written by historian and researcher Albert Manucy, it is on display in the Castillo de San Marcos.

For three years, 1875-1878, Indians from the western plains were confined in Fort Marion (Castillo de San Marcos). Zotom, a Kiowa Indian, became quite proficient in sketching the Fort, scenes on Anastasia Island, and views from the walls of the Fort. One of his sketches is shown on page 91. In 1886 -1887 Apaches were imprisioned at the Fort. During their year–long confinement, they introduced their native art style, creating many sketches and art works depicting their new environment.

Chapin's Handbook of St. Augustine, published in 1884, contains drawings by S. E. Brown. They are of particular interest since they were done just prior to Mr. Flagler's arrival in St. Augustine.

Flagler Era Artists' Colony

It was not until Mr. Flagler fashioned his opulent winter resort in the 1880s that artists found St. Augustine an exciting and productive winter home with enticements including a row of studios behind the luxurious Ponce de León Hotel. Mr. Flagler had hired Louis Comfort Tiffany (1848–1933) to do the interior design of the hotel. The magnificent stained glass windows of the Ponce de León Hotel increased the interest in his work. George W. Maynard (1843–1923) painted exquisite murals of gold, blue, and red tones, his symbolic figures filling the ceilings of the rotunda and dining hall. Angelic canvasses, painted by Virgilio Tojetti in Paris, covered the ceiling of the grand parlor and filled the spaces between ceiling moldings.

It was in this atmosphere that Mr. Flagler, a patron of the arts, constructed the row of seven studios. The second floor rooms faced Valencia Street with an open porch supported by palm tree columns. One of the first occupants was Martin Johnson Heade (1819–1904) who discovered Florida in the 1880s. His reputation as a landscape artist continued to spread during the years he occupied the seventh studio. Although his orchids, painted in their native setting in Brazil, drew much attention, his Cherokee roses, yellow jasmine, and orange blossoms were beautiful representations of the Florida environment. Mr. Heade, who eventually made St. Augustine his home, is perhaps the most notable of the colony's artists.

A versatile and popular artist who made use of space in studios one and two was Felix de Crano (?–1908). In addition to painting European scenes, flowers, and life studies, Mr. de Crano produced numerous views of St. Augustine sites. He painted scenes of the Fort, including interior views; the City Gate; landscapes of the beaches and the flats to the south. A large oil of the oldest house on St. Francis Street and a view of the Peck House on St. George Street are interesting depictions of the well–known buildings as they appeared in the 1890s. Mr. de Crano also became a St. Augustine resident. His three–story Colonial Revival home, known as "Shingles," was built at *44 Sevilla Street* before 1899 and is one of the fine residences near what was then the Ponce de León Hotel

William Staples Drown (1856–1915) was a prolific painter of St. Augustine views. An 1892 newspaper article noted that his pictures familiarized the quaint streets, picturesque houses, and pretty bits of the bay, sea wall, and old Fort to hundreds of persons who had never been there. Mr. Drown's views of the Ximenez–Fatio house, the Poujoud House (Sanchez House), and the bayfront are interesting representations of those sites in the late 19th century. Another resident of Artists' Row was George W. Seavey (?–1913), brother of Osburn D. Seavey who was then manager of the Ponce de León Hotel. George Seavey's floral renderings were popular works among the art colony's followers.

Other notables within the colony were Otto Bacher, Marie á Becket, Frank H. Shapleigh, and Laura Woodward. Mr. Bacher (1856–1909) was a well–known etcher who had exhibited in France and England. Of interest to St. Augustinians is his etching of the Ponce de León entrance. Marie á Becket (?–1904) focused on night scenes as subject matter for her paintings. Her landscapes in moonlight were fascinating studies and much admired by advocates of the Impressionist school. She was also a delightful entertainer and frequently told stories as she worked in her studio. Mr. Shapleigh (1842–1906) was a Bostonian as was his colleague, Mr. Seavey. Miss Woodward reproduced Florida scenery in both watercolor and oil. Her pictures made familiar many of the characteristics of the state. However, the talented artist did not stay in St. Augustine, rather she followed the migration of wealthy Northerners to Palm Beach.

In addition to Miss Woodward, two other women occupied studios in Artists' Row. Charlotte Buell Corman worked from number 5 for a time and provided space to Marion Foster sometime after 1900. Other names associated with the second floor studios include Arthur Callender who accompanied W. Staples Drown to St. Augustine in 1894 and opened his own studio the following season. In 1896 H. Anthony Dyer exhibited paintings whose subject was the effects of different times of day upon a scene. His St. Augustine views gave new perspective to familiar scenes. The animal paintings of J. H. Dolph drew admirers to the studio in 1910. Carl J. Blenner, J. W. Champney, and Robert S. German were among the artists who found St. Augustine a stimulating winter workshop and chose Artists' Row as their headquarters.

Highlights of the winter seasons of the 1890s were the regular Friday night receptions held in the artists' studios. At that time, the artists displayed their work in a pleasant and relaxed atmosphere. The studios were regarded among the attractive places of the city to visit, and the well attended Friday evening events were enjoyed by artists, art lovers, and those who simply came to socialize.

There were, of course, other artists of the period who found accommodations elsewhere. One of the earliest was William Akin Walker. Mr. Walker, a New Orleans native, painted southern plantation scenes. His work was exhibited in Tugby's, a popular shop on St. George Street. An artist who visited St. Augustine around the turn–of–the–century is described by *Tatler* only as Mrs. Evans of Chicago. She was a talented engraver who owned her own press and printed her own etchings to achieve the desired tones. One of Mrs. Evans' etchings was the door of Trinity Episcopal Church. Harry E. Graves, a Philadelphia artist, visited St. Augustine in 1896, noting that the narrow streets and period houses were worthy of the painter's brush. His exhibits were shown in a room of the Granada Hotel, although his primary work depicted the Ormond area, he did several studies of St. Augustine. An artist whose works were commissioned for buildings in Washington, D.C., was also an admirer of the Ancient City. H. S. Hilliard painted several views while visiting the city in the early 1900s. Two women, Mrs. L. Steele Kellogg and Mrs. Kemp–Welch were popular watercolor artists. Mrs. Kemp–Welch worked from her studio in the Valencia Hotel. Works by Heade, DeCrano, Drown and other artists of the era still exist in the Ancient City. The Lightner Museum exhibits some original works as does Flagler College. Others are in private collections.

Art in the 20th Century

The popularity of St. Augustine as an artists' colony waned as the winter tourist traffic pushed farther south. That does not mean, however, that interest in art diminished in the Ancient City. In July 1939, a *St. Augustine Record* article proclaimed that the city as an art colony was making rapid strides. By that time, the Galleon Arts Club, established in 1924, had evolved into the St. Augustine Arts Club. The group of artists, art lovers, and patrons was on firm footing by the time the article was printed. Local artists included Todd Lindenmuth, Elizabeth B. Warren (Mrs. Lindenmuth), Hildegarde Muller–Uri, and Celia Cregor Reid. They were among the enthusiastic supporters who had already established a following. Popular photographer Victor Rahner and *St. Augustine Record* editor Nina Hawkins rallied to the cause as well, encouraging the resurgence of an artists' colony in St. Augustine.

Today the St. Augustine Art Association has a fine permanent collection of art works produced over the decades and continues to support the current artists deserving recognition for their work in the city. Its collection contains works by the original founders of the Artists' Colony, but has none from the Flagler Era. The Association does, however, have works by well–known artists of the 1930s including Heinrich Pfeiffer, Walter Cole, and Louis Kronberg. New artists involved with the society recognized nationally and internationally include John McIver, J. Everett Draper, and Nan Greacon. In recent years the Art Association has grown from a membership of 150 to more than 600. The number of privately owned galleries in St. Augustine has tripled and outdoor art shows have increased at least two–fold. The original concept of St. Augustine as an artists' colony truly has been revitalized.

It took more than three centuries for artists to discover St. Augustine, and even longer for the city to be discovered through the art medium. The artists' colony which flourished in the 1890s is past history. Art, however, in St. Augustine is still very much present and all signs indicate it has a very good future.

Appendix 2.

Cemeteries

Every day tourists pass the Huguenot Cemetery on *San Marco Avenue* between *Orange Street and Castillo Drive*. Many also view the old tombstones beside La Leche Shrine on the Mission of Nombre de Dios grounds, and a few find their way to Tolomato Cemetery on *Cordova Street*. The earliest of these is Tolomato which opened in the early 1700s.

Evidence of 16th century Spanish cemeteries in the oldest portions of the town have been uncovered in several archaeological digs sponsored by the Historic St. Augustine Preservation Board. One of the earliest Spanish cemeteries was on Avilés Street near the site of the reconstructed Spanish Military Hospital.

Perhaps the most detailed archaeological research efforts have been made on the site of Nuestra Senora de la Soledad located on south St. George Street across from St. Joseph's Convent. Documented evidence has long indicated the presence of a parish church and a hospital on the site, the earliest mention made around 1597. In the 1970s archaeologists explored the site uncovering numerous skeletal remains, thus proving the existence of the cemetery as suspected. In addition to the Avilés Street, the Soledad burial grounds, and the Seloy Indian village burial site near the present day Fountain of Youth,other burial areas recorded include a site near St. Francis Barracks, one on the Cathedral-Basilica grounds, and one north of town in an area west of U.S. Highway One, north of State Road 16.

Tolomato Cemetery

Tolomato, which runs west of Cordova Street, just south of Orange Street, received its name from the "Church and Village of Tolomato," an Indian village depicted on a 1737 map. A map of 1764 describes a building there as a "little stone chapel of Our Lady of Guadalupe for the Tolomato Indians." The use of the property for burial of the Christian Indians was confirmed in a later document. The British probably did not use the cemetery during their occupancy from 1763 to 1784. However, it was used once again after the return of the Spanish. Gertrude Pons, who died on October 6, 1784, was the first official death recorded.

The use of the property as a cemetery was a distinct source of irritation to one city resident, Don Miguel Ysnardy. In a legal document drafted in 1799, Sr. Ysnardy petitioned Governor Enrique White to remedy a difficult situation. The problem? The cemetery sat in the middle of some newly acquired land that Sr.

Ysnardy wished to cultivate. He asked the governor to force the church to move the cemetery, claiming it not only precluded farming, but he repeatedly alleged the church was illegally charging for burials on his property. When Vicar Don Miguel O'Reilly learned of Sr. Ysnardy's charges, he responded with indignation. His lengthy retort included an explanation of the history of the property dating back to the days of the "old Spanish" who used the land for Christian Indian burials. He countered the charge of burial fees by stating that the pittance charged for funerals was an ecclesiastical fee unrelated to the burial plot. Without any legal document to support the church's right to use the land, Vicar O'Reilly put forth a good argument for maintaining the status quo. Although the judgment of the case was not recorded, the evidence of Vicar O'Reilly's success is clearly visible behind the Tolomato gates.

Tolomato Cemetery was officially closed in 1884; however, two interments occurred later. Mrs. Catalina Usina Llambias died in 1886 and Robert P. Sabate died in 1892. Both are buried in the cemetery, and in both cases family members paid a $25 fine for the illegal burial. Family tradition states that Joseph Francis Llambias fulfilled a death–bed promise to his mother, Catalina. Robert Sabate was laid to rest beside Mattie and Marcella Sabate. To both families, $25 probably was a small penalty to pay for the illegal acts.

The mortuary chapel at the rear of the cemetery contains the remains of Most Reverend Jean Pierre Augustin Marcellin Verot, the first bishop of St. Augustine. Prior to the Reverend Verot's death in 1876, the body of Father Felix Francisco Jose Maria de la Concepcion Varela was entombed in the chapel. Father Varela was a Havana–born member of the Spanish Cortes who was exiled from Spain for his pro–Cuban sentiments. He became vicar–general of the New York diocese and made frequent visits to St. Augustine. He died in St. Augustine in 1853, was buried in Tolomato Cemetery, and was later entombed in the mortuary chapel erected by his admirers.

A legend concerning Father Verot's burial states that Father Varela's bones were placed in a pillow case and moved to the rear of the vault to make room for Father Verot. Even with that, Father Varela was not yet able to rest in peace. In 1911 his remains were moved to Cuba where they were placed in a shrine honoring him as a national hero. The mortuary chapel was renovated prior to the 100th anniversary of Father Verot's death. The cemetery was also cleaned and landscaped for the commemorative ceremonies held in June 1976. During the 1980s repairs were made to tombstones and box tombs and a sculpture of Father Verot was created by St. Augustine artist Theodore Karem and placed in the center of the cemetery.

Closed now for nearly a century, the Tolomato Cemetery stands as a memorial to the people who shaped the community.

La Leche Cemetery

A small cemetery adjacent to La Leche Shrine on the Mission of Nombre de Dios grounds was operated primarily during the 1800s. The earliest recorded burial in La Leche Cemetery is 1856; however, the majority occurred between 1874 and 1891. A small walled area contains the remains of six Catholic sisters of the congregaton of St. Joseph who arrived in 1866 to teach.

Huguenot Cemetery

In July 1821 Florida became a United States possession, and with the influx of the new residents came the need for Protestant affiliations. Even before a church could be established, a cemetery was needed. An epidemic of yellow fever erupted within two months of the change of flags. The Catholic cemetery, Tolomato, was the only burial place. Protestants who lived in St. Augustine during late Spanish rule were buried on Anastasia Island. The practice would obviously not suffice in American–controlled St. Augustine. In short order the city council obtained permission from the federal government to open a half–acre plot outside the City Gate as a public burying ground. The cemetery satisfactorily served the purpose of a final resting place for non–Catholics, although the legitimacy of ownership was questioned by Lorenzo Capella, the last owner of the property in the Spanish period. The problem was resolved when Mr. Capella sold the plot to Thomas Alexander, the Presbyterian minister. In 1832 the land was legally transferred to the trustees of the church with the understanding that it would continue to serve as a burial ground for all Protestants. Although the property was returned to the city in the 1940s, it was quickly given back to the Presbyterian church. Today it remains the responsibility of the Trustees of Memorial Presbyterian Church.

The sign still displayed above the San Marco Avenue gate proclaims the burial ground to be a Huguenot Cemetery. The cemetery is sometimes referred to as the Public Burial Grounds to avoid the mistaken belief that the massacred Huguenots of the 1565 encounter with Menéndez are buried there; however, the Huguenot name has been retained for several reasons. It was referred to as the Huguenot Cemetery as early as 1832. It gained a reputation as a tourist interest with that name as early as the Flagler era. And, perhaps most importantly, recent research indicates that members of the Huguenot Church of Charleston, South Carolina, are buried there. Additionally, the close bonds of the Presbyterian and Huguenot religions, both followers of the religious reformer John Calvin, suggest the name could have been chosen by Presbyterians to memorialize the slain Frenchmen. The cemetery is now open to the public at posted times with new interpretive signs. It is currently undergoing restoration with partial aid from a state grant.

National Cemetery

St. Augustine can claim another first, or oldest, when discussing the National Cemetery on Marine Street. A proposal in 1881 resulted in the establishment of the first national military burial ground in Florida. This was accomplished approximately 20 years after President Abraham Lincoln approved legislation forming federal cemeteries for the war dead. Long before it was nationalized, the land beside St. Francis Barracks, now the Florida Department of Military Affairs and known as the Arsenal, was used for burials. The land, originally the property of a Franciscan monastery, has been used by the military from the late 18th century British occupation until the present. Although the British constructed wooden barracks on the land beside the monastery, the property west of the stone buildings was cleared during the early years of United States possession and declared a post cemetery. The first recorded interment was in 1818. Most of the early burials were soldiers who died during the Florida Indian wars. In 1842, with the advent of peace, it was determined to reinter all those who died within the territory, bringing them to one burial ground. Three pyramids at the south end of the cemetery cover vaults containing the remains of 1,468 war dead. This includes the more than 100 who died with Major Francis L. Dade, for whom the memorial is named. The obelisk in front of the pyramids was added in the 1880s when the cemetery was nationalized.

Improvements and additions over the years include the coquina wall, additional property designated for cemetery use in 1912 and 1913, and a superintendent's lodge constructed in 1938. The cemetery, which has been filled since the 1960s, displays a flag illuminated 24 hours a day. It became one of 10 national cemeteries to do this when first lighted in 1975.

Union soldiers at the Dade Memorial Pyramids in National Cemetery, ca. 1864

Appendix 3.

Family Businesses

During the early years, St. Augustine was almost completely dependent on the Spanish crown for subsistence. Slowly, family businesses began to emerge. A sampling of a few of these important family businesses is outlined, providing an interesting sidelight to a study of the city's heritage.

Cattle

As the little settlement neared its 100th birthday, a number of enterprising Spaniards determined that cattle raising could be a lucrative enterprise. During the last half of the 17th century the cattle industry flourished with the Menéndez Marques family a dominant force. The family, comprised of descendents of St. Augustine's founder, Pedro Menéndez de Avilés, owned ranches throughout northern Florida. The largest, La Chua, was located in present–day Alachua County. Closer to St. Augustine was the St. Johns River valley ranch near what is now Palatka. Another nearby ranch was Diego Plains in the vicinity of the present–day Ponte Vedra–Palm Valley communities. Don Diego de Espanosa operated the prosperous ranch, maintaining a hacienda there as late as 1740 when General James Oglethorpe's troops occupied the ranch. Although physical structures on the property were destroyed at that time, the excellent grazing land was unharmed, and the Espinosa family continued to raise cattle there. The ranch prospered for several generations under the management of the Espinosa–Sanchez family, a union formed by the marriage of Antonia Espinosa and José Sanchez de Ortigosa in 1756. Diego Plains may have been one of the last Spanish cattle ranching areas to survive the increasing threat of British encroachment on Spanish soil. Governor James Moore's raid in 1702 marked the end of prosperity for the industry which never recovered after the devastating attack.

Citrus

By the mid–1700s oranges were a cash crop, with exportation to the British colonies to the north bolstering the economy. A second mid–century product came from the abundant forest of the St. Johns River valley. Naval stores (resin, turpentine, pitch, and tar) were in great demand. During British occupancy, exportation of oranges continued, but it was the indigo industry which proved most profitable to the crown. By the end of the Revolutionary War, Florida was the leading exporter of the plant to Britain's thriving industrial market. The orange industry remained a primary money–maker after the return of the Spanish. Once again the forest products, particularly timber, provided another means of income for the Spanish and American families living in Florida. The 37 years of Spanish rule, however, were not a time of prosperity. As the Spanish realized the imminent loss of the Florida province, they were little motivated to develop new businesses. It was left to the American newcomers to find an industry that suited the little settlement.

Tourism

It was not long after the United States took possession of Florida in 1821 that word spread of the healthful effects of the warm climate. Winter visitors soon appeared about town seeking comfortable accommodations. The only hostelry existing before 1835 was the Union Hotel, which had been converted from a residence by its owner, William Livingston, and his daughter, Hester. Boarding houses and private homes soon opened their doors to winter guests, thus providing a new source of income for enterprising residents. Without the label "tourism" used today, St. Augustine's primary industry began. In 1835 the Florida Hotel opened and in 1847 the Magnolia Hotel followed suit. The Civil War years curtailed the growing business. The 1870s saw a resurgence of interest in the city's climate and by the 1880s the city was entering the golden age of the Flagler Era.

An interesting and charming tourist–related business prevalent today originated in the early 1880s and has remained in family hands for more than a century. The founder of the St. Augustine Transfer Company was Louis A. Colee, a native of St. Augustine whose family ran the stage coach line between St. Augustine and Picolata. The Colee business consisted of a variety of carriages including Landaus for funeral processions. Louis Colee gave Mr. Flagler his first look at the Ancient City. As Mr. Flagler's enterprises expanded, so did Mr. Colee's. His omnibuses and Phaetons met all trains to transport the winter visitors to their hotels. With the advent of the automobile, the Transfer Service was modified. For a time the Colee family invested in automobiles and trucks, but soon the old carriages and horses, which occasionally sported hats or ear muffs, became a quaint and pleasant aspect of the city's growing tourist industry.

Colee's Carriages continue to transport visitors

Still under Colee family management, the business is considered the oldest enterprise in St. Augustine continuously operated by one family.

The Flagler era propelled the tourist industry to the pinnacle of economic importance in St. Augustine. Prior to the formation of the Flagler enterprises, the town of 2,500 residents contained eight boarding houses, three restaurants, and 18 dry goods/general merchandise shops. By 1889, the growing town had 12 hotels and 45 dry goods/general merchandise shops. There were still only three locally operated restaurants indicating that competition from the hotel dining rooms discouraged investment in business ventures of this type. Three curiosity shops were added to the previous number, bringing the total to nine. Eleven real estate companies blossomed in the boom town. As St. Augustine prospered, established businessmen such as Bartolo Genovar, T. W. Speissegger, and C. F. Hamblen continued to expand, benefiting from the rapidly developing tourist industry.

Retailing

Bartolo Genovar, known as the "prince of merchants," was a St. Augustine native whose family ties to the city dated from 1777. He developed a business in the 1860s dealing in provisions, groceries, liquors, and orange growing. As the economy prospered, Mr. Genovar expanded to include real estate and banking and then added politics to his many activities. The Genovar family also contributed significantly to the entertainment field, opening the first theater capable of housing large touring companies. The Genovar Opera House, originally located on Charlotte Street, burned in 1914; however, prior to that time it provided a source of pleasure for visitors and residents alike for many years, and was subsequently replaced by a new hall.

T. W. Speissegger and Sons Druggists was a company well–established by the Flagler Era. Begun in the early 1870s, the business was forced to relocate after a fire burned the Bayfront store in 1887. The new store at *31 Orange Street* handled a complete line of drugs, patent medicines, toilet and fancy articles, tobacco, and cigars. The building now serves as a museum commemorating the early family business begun by Mr. Speissegger and continued by his sons T. Julius and R. A. until the 1960s.

C. F. Hamblen also profited from the growing economy of the 1880s and 1890s. His general merchandising business was ready and waiting when Mr. Flagler began building. Mr. Hamblen modified the company, specialized in hardware, and provided many of the building needs of the developing community. Now considered one of the oldest businesses in St. Augustine, it, too, is commemorated by a museum operating from the final location of the Hamblen Hardware Store at *4 Artillery Lane.*

Cigar Manufacturing

The first factory in St. Augustine to commercially produce cigars was established by Bartolo and Frank Genovar. The factory opened before the turn of the century and was located in a large frame building on Charlotte Street between Treasury and Hypolita streets.

It was, however, P. F. Carcaba who lent the greatest impetus to the industry. Sr. Carcaba, a native of Spain, opened his factory on Hypolita Street and began a thriving business. An expert in his field, he frequently traveled to Cuba to purchase select leaves for his cigars. Popular brands marketed by his company were El Mas Nobel, Merciless, La Flor de P.F.C. y Co., La Perla, Espanola, and Neptuno. Although the heart of the Florida tobacco industry was centered in the Tampa area, Sr. Carcaba chose to remain in St. Augustine and inspired a son and son–in–law to continue cigar production. His son, William, and son–in–law, Augustine Solla, teamed with Antonio Martinez to organize a new company. They purchased the interests of William Genovar and located the business in the old Genovar factory on Charlotte Street.

The newly named firm of Martinez, Solla, and Carcaba appeared to have a bright future and every effort was made to guarantee its success. A parcel of land at *88 Riberia Street* was donated for construction of a factory, and between 1907 and 1910, a four–story brick building arose with great promise. The company never achieved its predicted success. William Carcaba was killed in a tragic accident and his partner, Mr. Solla died soon after. Mr. Martinez moved to Jacksonville to pursue business interests there. The cigar manufacturing firm of Pamies and Arrango moved to the large factory on Riberia Street after the Martinez, Solla, Carcaba firm ceased to function. They successfully produced their product until 1929 when the factory closed. The large building has been restored for office use in recent years.

Another important cigar making firm was La Usina Cigar Company. Frederick C. Usina began cigar manufacturing just before the turn–of–the–century and maintained his business until the 1920s. La Usina Cigar Company produced a cigar named Lynola, perhaps inspired by Mrs. Usina's first name, Leonilla.

Shrimping

In the 1920s three Italian families arrived in St. Augustine to establish another industry that helped fill the void left by the declining cigar industry. The pioneers of the St. Augustine shrimping industry, Salvador Versaggi, Anthony Poli, and Sollecito Salvador brought knowledge and experience gained from two decades of shrimping in Fernandina Beach. The industry grew rapidly, and by the 1940s there were 100 ships operating out of St. Augustine. At that time shrimping ranked as the fourth largest industry in the county. Unfortunately, the precarious industry still fluctuates as shrimp change location, and environmental regulations require expensive modifications. Although not a major industry, shrimp boats can be seen passing through the Bridge of Lions every day.

Twentieth Century Businesses

Many small family–operated businesses have continued to survive over the decades. Henry W. Davis opened a clothing store on King Street in 1894. The men's shop still operates from the original location in the Cordova block. Eugene L. Barnes and Sons Insurance Company was established in 1895 as Canfield and Barnes. The founder's grandson operated the company from a King Street office until the mid–1980s when he moved the business to its present Valencia Street location. For years, M. Altoonjian and Company sold wares from a shop located in the Cordova block. Formed in the early 1900s as an outlet for Oriental goods, Altoonjian's existed until recent years.

Black-operated businesses in the 1920s and 1930s included: Home Circle Publishing Company, James Reddick, editor; Sanitary House Cleaning Company owned by the Welters Brothers; Iceberg Ice Cream Company owned by Forward and DeLarge; and West Side Dry Cleaning owned by Boyd W. Smith. Perhpas the best known businessman was Frank B. Butler (1885-1973) who owned the Palace Market on Washington Street and was president of College Park Realty Company.

Some family businesses have been maintained by the women of the household. Such is the case with Lila Snow who managed her husband's real estate firm after his death around 1920. She formed a partnership with her son and renamed the business Lila M. Snow and Son. From the 1920s until 1964 Dorothy Parker Dewhurst ran the St. Johns County Abstract Company, a business organized by her father, William W. Dewhurst. A third woman, Edith Pomar, became president of her late husband's business, the J. N. Pomar Metal Company in the early 1930s.

Appendix 4.

Monuments and Memorials

Statues

Statues are among the most prominent reminders of a city's founders and significant residents. Each represents an individual important to the history of the community.

Although neither a resident nor a founder, the small statue of Isabella de Catolica, Queen Isabella of Spain, serves as the focal point of the Hispanic Gardens in the restored area of St. George Street. The Queen is honored for her support of Christopher Columbus' exploration of the new world. The bronze, sculpted by Anna Huntington, was placed in the garden in 1965.

Don Juan Ponce de León has looked north from his spot on the waterfront east of the Plaza since 1923. The statue, a gift of Dr. Andrew Anderson, replicates a statue of Ponce de León which stands beside the explorer's grave in San Juan, Puerto Rico.

Don Pedro Menéndez de Avilés, the city's founding father, overlooks the front garden of the Lightner Museum/City Hall Complex at *75 King Street*. The bronze statue was erected in 1972. It was presented to St. Augustine by Mayor Fernando Juarez of Avilés, Spain, as a gift from the sister city. The garden area was formally dedicated as Parque de Menéndez in 1979.

On the grounds of the Mission of Nombre de Dios stands the 11–foot tall bronze statue of Father Francisco Lopez de Mendoza Grajales. The replica of the Spanish priest was sculpted by Yugoslavian artist Ivan Mestrovic. The statue, and the 208–foot stainless steel cross to the east mark the site of Menéndez' landing and the celebration of the first mass which Father Lopez, as fleet chaplain, led. The mission cross, designed by Eugene F. Kennedy, Jr., was erected on the grounds in 1966.

The Memorial to Father Pedro Camps is located in the Cathedral Courtyard. It was a gift of Xavier L. Pellicer and a resident of Minorca, Dr. Fernando Rubio. The memorial was erected in 1975 and commemorates the spiritual leader of the New Smyrna colonists as well as the families who migrated to St. Augustine in 1777. It was sculpted by Barcelona artist, Joseph Viladomat.

In front of Flagler Colege is the bronze likeness of Henry Morrison Flagler. The statue of the oil and railroading magnate was constructed in 1915 and moved to its present site in the early 1970s.

Many of the city's monuments are located in the Plaza.

The **Spanish Public Well** is a reconstruction of a Spanish
period well which was filled and partially destroyed
during the British Period. Part of a 1975 bicentennial project,
it represents one of the most recent contributions to the Plaza area.

The **Constitution Obelisk** was erected in 1814 to celebrate the
newly formed constitutional government in Spain. For a time, when the
government was overturned, the plaque was removed. It was replaced
on the 30–foot monument in 1920 and proclaimed the area as the
"Plaza de la Constitucion."

The **Confederate War Memorial Obelisk** was commissioned
by the Ladies' Memorial Association was headed by Anna Dummett,
sister–in–law of Confederate General William J. Hardee. Erected in
1872, it was originally located on the east side of St. George
Street, then moved to just west of the Market Place.

The **World War II Memorial Monument** honors St. Johns
County residents who died in World War II. The plaque and
monument are just north of the Market Place. The memorial was
presented to the city by the Pilot Club in 1946. The names of those
who lost their lives in Korea and Vietnam have been added.

The **Felix Francisco Jose Maria de la Concepcion Varela
Monument** commemorates the Cuban–born Patriot–Priest.

Located in a small park on the western side of Government House is the
William Wing Loring Memorial to the City. Presented by the Daughters of the
Confederacy in 1920, the pillar commemorates Confederate General Loring for his
gallantry during the Civil War and for military service during the Seminole Indian
conflict.

Within the National Cemetery on Marine Street there is a trio of pyramids
and an accompanying tall obelisk. The vaults beneath the pyramids contain the
remains of 1,468 men who died during the Florida Indian Wars (1835–1842). The
grave markers are generally known as the Dade Memorial, commemorating the first
100 men who died with their commander, Major Francis L. Dade, at the massacre
marking the beginning of the Seminole War.

The World War I Flagpole was dedicated in 1921 and is located in front of the American Legion Building at *One Anderson Circle* on the Bayfront. It was a gift of Dr. Andrew Anderson, a physician who served three terms as county commissioner in the 1870s and mayor from 1886–1887.

There are memorials, statues, parks, and old wells. Are they vital to appreciate the heritage of the city? Consider this: In 1900 the city fathers proposed to demolish the cracking City Gate, which was then 92–years–old. The persistence of a dedicated group of women saved the landmark. It is difficult to imagine St. George Street without the coquina pillars that have marked the northern entrance of the Ancient City since 1808. The location at the north end of the street is significant since the original northern access to the walled city had also been through a gate. The first gate had been built on the site in 1739 when an entryway was incorporated into the defense system.

The Bridge of Lions with its noble marble guardians is the draw bridge has spanned the Matanzas River since 1917. The old world appearance of the four Mediterranean Revival towers adds a distinctive dimension to the Ancient City. The aesthetic attributes of the pair of lions were a gift from Dr. Andrew Anderson and were sculpted by F. Romanelli of Florence, Italy, modeled after the pair of lions guarding the Loggia Dei Lanzi in Florence.

A portion of the seawall built by the Spanish is still standing. The section nearest the Castillo de San Marcos was part of an early wall that extended from the Fort to the Plaza. An extension from the Plaza south to St. Francis Barracks, now the National Guard Arsenal, was added by the US Army between 1835 and 1842.

There are two interesting objects in the courtyard of the Lightner Museum/ City Hall Complex. The Coats Bridge is a rubblework stone walking bridge designed and erected in 1948 by N. Frances Coats of Floral City, Florida. It crosses the pool and overlooks O.C. Lightner's marble gravestone. Mr. Lightner, the founder of *Hobbies* magazine bequeathed a large collection of Victorian memorabilia displayed in the museum that bears his name.

To the north of the Florida East Coast Railway building at *One Malaga Street* is the little Railroad Park built between 1885 and 1894. The park was originally surrounded by the depot and other railroad buildings.

In St. Augustine, each monument, site, memorial, park, and object represents the special character of the city and serves as a continuing reminder of the area's heritage.

Appendix 5

Streets

Although St. Augustine is a relatively easy city to navigate, it becomes more complex when considering the evolution, pronunciation, and placement of its streets over the past 400 years. For example, there are a few street names, such as Hypolita, where correct pronunciation is a challenge for the uninitiated. Is the name Hi–pol'–i–ta or is it Hee–pol–ee'–ta? If one wishes to give Saint Hypolita the proper Spanish pronunciation, it should be the latter with an accent on the next to last syllable and with a silent "H." Incidentally, the present Hypolita Street was formerly Calle Real, Saint Patrick Street, and Partner's Lane. Today's Spanish Street was the original "Hippolyte" or Saint Hypolita Street before evolving into Dragoon Street or Street of the Dragoon Barracks.

Another tongue–twister is found in the name of a street just south of the Florida School for the Deaf and the Blind. Genoply (Jen–o–ply') sounds like layers of a towel–something between one–ply and two–ply. Residents know it is pronounced Jen–op'–o–ly for Juan Genopoly, an important early settler whose name appears to have been spelled several different ways. A little south of Genoply Street is a road running from San Marco Avenue to U.S. Highway One (also known as Ponce de León Boulevard).

The street, spelled Rhode for years, commemorates Henry Rohde, a land developer who subdivided property in the general vicinity of Cincinnati and Rhode streets. A newspaper article written around the mid–1930s announced the approaching visit of Captain Boerge Rohde of the Danish Royal Life Guards and his bride, Mrs. Ruth Bryan Owen, U.S. Minister to Denmark. A motorcade was planned to escort the couple down the street that bore the Rohde family name. Fortunately, the street name was spelled correctly at the time. While the street name's spelling was later changed to Rhode (as in Rhode Island), the pronunciation has remained Ro–dee, presenting a somewhat confusing situation for residents and newcomers alike. Recently the sign was changed back to read Rohde Street.

Interesting street names in the North City section include Hope and Bernard. Hope is not, as one might suspect, of sentimental derivation. The street was named for two homeowners on the block, Holmes and Perry, who combined the first two initials of both names to form Ho–Pe or Hope Street. F. J. Holmes was the owner of the city ice–works and Joe Perry served as Sheriff of St. Johns County. Bernard Street should logically be named for Bernard Masters, a member of the Masters (Maestre) family who migrated to the city from New Smyrna in 1777. Mr. Masters developed the area surrounding the present Bernard Street, building many large frame houses including the building at *102 San Marco Avenue,* now the Raintree Restaurant. Although the Masters Tract takes its name from the prolific builder, relatives do not believe he named Bernard Street for himself. As a young man, Bernard Masters worked in the shipyards in Savannah, Georgia. He retained fond memories of that city and of the street on which he lived, Bernard Street. Many of the streets in North City were named for well–known local families. Sanchez Street represents the first Spanish period family; Perpall and Genovar Streets are named for New Smyrna colony immigrants. Vedder Street is named for the Vedder family, probably best known in St. Augustine for the Dr. John Vedder Museum on Bay Street which contained exhibits of natural history, ancient maps, and relics. Another family member, Elihu Vedder was a distinguished artist.

Garnett Avenue memorializes Dr. Ruben B. Garnett whose magnificent orange grove was located between St. Louis and San Sebastian avenues, now the location of motels, a gas station, and a super market. Mr. Garnett donated land to the Catholic Church for the purpose of constructing St. Agnes School, still located on San Sebastian Avenue. Dismukes Street is named for the family headed by John T. Dismukes, a bank president and civic–minded citizen. Nelmar Street, like Hope Street, is a combined form of two names: Nellie and Mary Fuller. The two women were the daughters of land developer Charles M. Fuller whose surname appears in the Fullerwood Street name.

In Abbott Tract there was much indecisiveness regarding street names. Abbott Street began as Washington, and Osceola was originally called Orange Street. Water Street was Cleland for a time, named for John C. Cleland, one of the land developers during the early growth of Abbott Tract. A move to rename the street Perry Place for Roscoe Perry, also an early resident of the street, was almost successful as evidenced in the 1886–1887 City Directory. Mr. Perry lists his home on Cleland Street, while his neighbors on the same thoroughfare claim to live on Perry Place. In later years the roadway became Water Street for its proximity to the North River and Matanzas Bay.

The southern–most strip of Abbott Tract appears on late 19th century maps and deeds as Clinch Street, probably named for Army General Duncan L. Clinch, a land speculator in the early 1880s and 1890s. Confusion arose regarding the exact property line dividing the tract from federally owned Fort Marion (the Castillo de San Marcos as renamed by the Americans). Eventually it was determined that the strip of land along which the street ran encroached on federal property and the thoroughfare disappeared along with Clinch's name. The neighboring street, now called Shenandoah, was named for Peter Skenandoah Smith. His memory was erased by the substitution of "H" for "K" which left a street name that conjures thoughts of rolling hills and valleys rather than the colorful land speculator. One street north of Shenandoah is Joiner Street. Perhaps the name is meant to indicate a thoroughfare joining east Abbott Tract with west; however, land developer, Joshua Joyner, would probably resent that conclusion.

The street running along the western boundary of Abbott Tract has the distinction of being one of the oldest roads outside the colonial city. At one time the road was known as the Mil y Quinientas. In later years the road was given the names Shell Road and the Public Road to Jacksonville. Both names have obvious derivations. For many years shell was the primary paving material used on this thoroughfare. As late as World War I, new crops of oysters were spread over the road. When the weather became hot and dry, the repercussions were disastrous. Live oysters trapped inside the shells smelled and white powder from the crushed shells permeated the air. A horse drawn wagon equipped with water sprinklers solved the latter problem, but no remedy was discovered to alleviate the stench created by the decaying mollusks.

For visitors or residents with an ear for Spanish verbiage, many of the city's street names have a familiar ring. Avilés (formerly Hospital Street) is named for the Spanish coastal town where the city's founder, Pedro Menéndez de Avilés, lived. Numerous streets such as Cadiz and Granada were assigned names of Spanish provinces and cities. Cadiz, changed from Green Street after the 1930s, also bore the romantic name Garden Lane as well as the indelicate appellation Grogg Lane. Bronson Street was changed to Granada around 1888. The street was probably named originally for Dr. Oliver Bronson, although winter resident, Robert Donaldson Bronson, and Judge Isaac Bronson could share the honor.

Almost all the streets in Model Land Tract followed the practice of imitating Spanish city names. Tolomato became Cordova when Henry M. Flagler began planning the construction of his luxury hotels. As the adjacent lands developed, the newly planned streets were either changed (Oleander became Sevilla) or assigned new foreign sounding labels. With few exceptions the area reads like a Spanish road map: Valencia, Almeria, Saragossa, Malaga, and Ovieda. The Spanish cities were generally the capitals of provinces and shared the name with the large area in which they were located; thus, the street names are Spanish provinces as well as cities. Unfortunately some of the names were "lost in translation." Oviedo became Ovieda and Zaragoza became Saragossa. Cordova should, by rights, be Cordoba. Valencia replaced another Spanish name, Alameda, which means grove or lane of elms, and does appear as the name of some Spanish towns, although no major city or province bears the name.

An interesting quandary arises when debating the origin of the name Riberia. Not only does it appear with two different spellings, Riberia, north of King Street, and Ribera to the south, but there is no such city in Spain. The closest in spelling is a small port town named Riberira. If one considers the spelling Ribera to be the correct form, the word translates to mean shoreline, an interesting possibility since Riberia Street formed the eastern limits of the San Sebastian River until Mr. Flagler filled in the marshes in the mid–1880s. Perhaps the street was intended to be Iberia, the name of the peninsula which Spain and Portugal occupy. Could some uninformed person have added the "R"? The origin of Carrera Street is another unanswered question. The street name could be a misspelling of John M. Carreré the architect whose name should correctly be pronounced Ca–rer without a third syllable. It is, however, frequently pronounced Carer–a as is the street name. Of course the street could be translated as "the race," the Spanish meaning of the word; however, it is difficult to imagine the road as a raceway, wide though it is. Other Spanish names such as La Quienta also are of dubious origin. The translation is "the fifth" (the fifth what?) or "the grand plantation," which is difficult to imagine in the particular location.

Pronunciation and derivation aside, the custom of using Spanish names and words to name streets has continued into present times. Davis Shores and other Anastasia Island communities include streets named Arredondo, Avista, Miruela, Gerardo, Andeas, Salamanca, Hermoso, Barcelona, and many more. Although some are misspelled (Corunna should be Coruna with a tilde over the "n"), the tradition remains strong.

Once can see the proverbial pendulum swing with the spate of Spanish names. Almost every street in colonial St. Augustine was at some time labeled "Calle Real" which translates as "Royal Street" but, in reality, is simply a designation of a public thoroughfare. Before Bay Street became Avenida Menéndez and Castillo Drive, it was known as Calle de la Marina (street of the sea) and La Playa (the beach). The name change to Avenida Menéndez was the suggestion of Mr. McCormick–Goodheart, a native of Alexandria, Virginia, who felt a strong bond to the Ancient City. He felt the newly widened street should honor the city's founder.

Some Spanish names pique one's curiosity. Cuna Street was once Lane de la Saya or Las Naguask, both of which translate to Petticoat Lane. Other more mundane names of that street have included Baker's Lane and Cradle Street. Treasury Street was once called Paniagua (bread and water) Lane. Charlotte Street was the street of the merchants, La Calle de Los Mercaderes, in 1764. Charlotte Street and St. George Street also appeared with the Spanish form of the current name, San Carlos or Carlota, and San Jorge. Cordova, which was Tolomato Street for a time, also bore the name of La Cienega (street of the swamp). Tolomato Lane was assigned the descriptive English name of Cemetery Lane, which was not as colorful as the Spanish name, Calle de Cuerpo Santo (the Street of the Body of the Saint).

Many other streets in colonial St. Augustine have undergone name changes. Marine Street probably sets the record with a list of names consisting of Broad Street, Street of the Barracks, St. Joseph Street, Juno Street, and Sacrament Street. Fort Lane was once Hog Lane. King Street was Government House Lane and Picolata Street, while Artillery Lane was known as Fare Lane or the awkward label of "The Cross Street of the Hospital." Bravo Lane has been called at various times Edmiston or Bosquet Lane. Bridge Street, named for the bridge across Maria Sanchez Creek was also Cunningham Lane and St. Joseph Street. St. Francis, too, had a variety of labels. It was sometimes known as Convent Lane, other times, Barracks Street or Royal Road.

Another feature of St. Augustine's streets, was the varied building materials. Early photographs show that most of the streets were dirt. Shell was used on some outlying roadways. A photograph dating from the 1880s shows men laying cypress wood blocks on Cathedral Place. Although the use of the blocks was not widespread, "wooden" streets did appear in other areas of the city. As late as 1925 cypress blocks could be seen on the north end of Malaga which had been covered with the material as far north as Almeria Street.

Sometime toward the end of the 19th century it was deemed necessary to cover the major thoroughfares of the city. Since coquina was the only indigenous stone, it was necessary to import adequate building material. Although brick had never been popular, it was the sensible choice. As major streets, such as St. George and Charlotte were bricked, the material was also used around the luxury hotels and in the newly developed Model Land Tract north of the Ponce de León Hotel. By 1913 a portion of Sevilla Street in front of the Memorial Presbyterian Church had been bricked. Names imprinted in many of the bricks included Southern Clay Mfg. Co., Reynolds Block, and Graves, B'ham, Ala. The manufacturers apparently provided satisfactory service as the same companies supplied the bricks for the extensive county roadway known as the Dixie Highway. The nine–foot wide highway was built between 1914 and 1917 and extended from St. Augustine to a point beyond Hastings.

In addition to its brick streets, St. Augustine contains some unique and interesting brick sidewalks. A photograph taken about the time of the opening of the Ponce de León Hotel in January 1888 shows Cordova and King streets unpaved, but with a neatly laid sidewalk beside the Alcazar. The decorative bricks, with straight lines accenting the shape, and circles in the center, were undoubtedly a Flagler inspiration. Distinctive sidewalks border many Flagler buildings and extend into areas of the colonial city. The sidewalks on both sides of St. George Street near St. Joseph Academy, still display the attractive bricks.

Two conclusions can be reached from a study of St. Augustine's streets. First, street names are subject to change. Some of the changes within the past half century have included: Venancio to Park Place, a section of St. Francis to Park Place. Cemetery Lane to San Salvador, Cyprian to Lovett, Ferry to Kings Ferry Way, Hamblen to Anderson Circle, Hernandez to Charlotte Place, and Hernandez to Tremerton, Wilmuth became East Lane, Worley was changed to Arenta, and St. John Street to DeHaven Street. Second, street names were misspelled. Genoply, Rohde, Joiner, and Shenandoah have been discussed. A fifth misspelling is Ingram Street which was named for the Ingraham family. The street, in Lighthouse Park, marks the location of the Ingraham family summer cottage. A few less flagrant errors generally go almost unnoticed such as the "s" being dropped from San Marco(s) Avenue. However, as long as residents know where they are going, and can point visitors in the right direction, such errors seem relatively insignificant.

Brick-lined streets add charm to St. Augustine

Appendix 6.

Walls

Walls, defined here as upright structures used to enclose property, are not an often-heard topic of conversation. What about the walls of St. Augustine? Of what possible consequence are the masonry fences that frequently make driving so difficult in some parts of the Ancient City? Not so surprisingly, there is a lot more to "walls" than meets the eye.

On Avilés Street near the intersection of Cadiz look closely at the coquina that forms part of the wall around St. Joseph's Convent at *241 St. George Street*. Careful inspection reveals marks showing outlines of doors or windows. Also visible are corner joints and ashlar scoring in the stucco, remnants of an 18th century house that once stood on that corner. The house, once called the Cavedo House, was constructed sometime before 1763. It was a one–story masonry dwelling with a flat roof and a side entrance from a loggia. It later became the residence of Juan Cavedo, a Minorcan who was a teen–ager when he arrived in St. Augustine in 1777 with the immigrants from the New Smyrna colony. By 1786 Juan was living in the house on the corner of Cadiz and Avilés with his wife, Juana Sequi, and his mother, Inez Victori. A room in the house was used as Sr. Cavedo's tailor shop. A photograph in the late 19th century indicates that the southern portico, or possibly a room, which appeared on the 1788 Rocque map disappeared by that time. A smaller structure, possibly the kitchen, was located on the south boundary of the lot and appeared to have been used for storage in later years. Both of the colonial structures, except for the existing walls, were torn down between 1904 and 1910.

The wall around St. Joseph's Convent of which the Cavedo House ruins are a part, continues south on Avilés Street to connect with the colonial buildings known as the O'Reilly House and Don Toledo House. On the St. George Street side is a portion of the wall constructed from coquina rock taken from a building once used as the first black school in St. Augustine. The building, a two–story residence, was used by Father Juan Nepomuceno Gomez as a parish school in 1816 and for several years thereafter. In 1866 the Sisters of St. Joseph opened it as a free school for blacks. It stood beside the main entrance to the convent. The vine–covered wall curves away from the street to open into the academy complex.

The ornate cast concrete wall in front of *262 St. George Street* has an interesting ecumenical history. It is a portion of a wall built in 1890 in front of the Cathedral and the Bishop's residence on Cathedral Place. In 1965, when the residence was razed, the fence was moved to its present location. The wall which for years encircled the Catholic Church and Bishop's home, now stands on the site of the First Presbyterian Church. The Protestant house of worship existed on the lot from 1824 until 1893.

Although the old Alencia Hotel was demolished in the 1960s, the 1890s wall survives. The poured concrete retaining wall was constructed when the hotel was built by J. A. McGuire, a partner in the McGuire and McDonald contracting firm which erected many Flagler buildings and hotels. The coquina and concrete wall rises about two–and–a–half feet from the sidewalk.

The coquina concrete block wall curving around the corner of Artillery Lane and St. George Street was constructed around 1901. It rises approximately four feet in height with a gate post raised a foot above. Ornamental capstones decorate the length of the wall and the gateposts. Notable as a late example of coquina construction in the city is part of the fence originally surrounding the Bigelow house, a two–story coquina and wooden structure built during the Flagler Era. Across from the Bigelow wall is a tabby wall dating from the mid–18th century. It is the only extant colonial tabby wall in St. Augustine. It forms the southern boundary of one of the oldest houses in the city at *214 St. George Street*. The wall extends about 15 feet west with a coquina section abutting the original tabby. Some sections are plastered and scored.

On the corner of Bridge and Marine streets is a wall that once surrounded the palatial residence of P. F. Carcaba, a prominent St. Augustinian successful in a cigarmaking enterprise. The three foot poured concerete wall constructed around 1900 was later doubled in height. There are two gates on the Marine Street side; one was evidently for pedestrians and the other for automobiles. The pedestrian gate has a poured concrete top on it. Along the Bridge Street side, the lower half of the wall is made with large coquina blocks with poured concrete on the upper half.

A wall that is now incorporated into the Monson Motel was once part of an old coquina dwelling on the corner of Treasury Street and what is now Avenida Menéndez. The house was owned in 1763 by Antonio Rodriguez Afrian, a militia lieutenant. In the late 18th century, it was the home of John Leslie of the influential trading firm, Panton, Leslie and Company. It was destroyed in the 1914 fire after serving for a time as the Vedder Museum.

Walls may never become a popular conversational topic, but they stand as important reminders of the city's heritage. Particularly in the Ancient City, they often combined defense and decoration, thereby greatly adding to the stability, security, and serenity of the residents.

Appendix 7.

Women

During the first two decades of the 20th century women owned or operated 80% of the city's boarding houses and 30% of the smaller hotels. During the Florida land boom of the 1920s, 70% of the female population was employed primarily in educational fields. In 1914 Julie Masters was listed as a stripper, a tobacco stripper in a cigar factory. In 1934 the local bug exterminator was Mrs. Janie Lawhorn whose office was on Cuna Street. These little known facts, compiled from early city directories, reflect a portion of the wealth of information gathered about women in St. Augustine.

When considering the women of the city, specific names are mentioned frequently. Sometimes it is women of prominent families such as Clarissa Anderson, Elizabeth Gibbs Webb, or Anna Burt. Educators such as Leone Roode, Jessie Avril, Evelyn Hamblen and Maude Shorter come to mind as do Edith Taylor Pope, and Elizabeth Ketterlinus. Within this section, the focus is primarily on St. Augustine women from the period spanning early statehood through the Civil War. Accomplishments of most 19th century women were family–oriented since occupational opportunities outside the home were scarce. Anna and Sarah Dummett operated the St. Francis Inn at 279 St. George Street. It is interesting to note that owning or managing a boarding house was one of the few suitable and lucrative occupations available to women in the mid–1800s.

An excellent example of work in the field was the all–woman administration of the Ximenez–Fatio House at *20 Avilés Street*. Purchased by Margaret Cook in 1830, the house was remodeled into a boarding house and operated as such until 1875. Mrs. Cook was assisted by Elizabeth C. Whitehurst, a widow. In 1838 the boarding house was sold to Sara Petty Anderson who continued the business until Louisa Fatio purchased the house in 1855. Mrs. Fatio's boarding house flourished for 20 years. After her death in 1875, the property was inherited by a nephew, Fatio Dunham. Today, the building is once again run by women, the Society of the Colonial Dames.

Mrs. Anderson and her friends Julia Gibbs, Frances Smith, and Anna Dummett were familiar figures throughout the Civil War. Although their sentiments were divided, the ladies remained cordial during the difficult years, perhaps because of their shared loyalty to their city. Mrs. Anderson consistently supported the Union. Mrs. Dummett was a staunch supporter of the Confederacy. She was also proprietor of the St. Francis Inn at 279 St. George Street and was responsible for the Confederate

War Memorial located in the Plaza. The St. Augustine chapter of the Daughters of the Confederacy was named in her honor. Mrs. Dummett maintained her British citizenship and her strong Confederate loyalty until her death in 1899.

Mrs. Smith, mother of Confederate General Edmund Kirby-Smith, was so outspoken about her Southern sentiments that she was exiled from the Union-occupied city in 1863. It is believed that while entertaining Union soldiers in her home at *12 Avilés Street* she was actually performing duties as a spy. The home in which she lived is now called the Sequi-Kirby Smith house and is being restored under the supervision of the St. Augustine Historical Society. The building was also the home of the first federal judge, Joseph Lee Smith, and the birth place of the Smith's son, Edmund.

Julia Williams Gibbs fled the city with her children as the Civil War drew to a close. The family was reunited in St. Augustine when her husband, Confederate Colonel George Couper Gibbs, was exonerated from war crime charges. Although the house they occupied on Marine Street has not survived, the site is now the location of the St. Augustine Art Center at 22 Marine Street. Numerous Gibbs descendants continue to live in St. Augustine.

A legendary figure who emerged after the war years was Lola Sanchez who, with her two sisters, relayed information about Union activities to the confederate soldiers. A dangerous night ride by Lola inspired a Paul Revere-like legend. The Sanchez home was in the western part of St. Johns County. One sister, Eugenia, did move to the city and lived at *61 Hypolita Street* after marrying Albert C. Rogero.

As St. Augustine rebuilt and expanded in the 1870s, a spunky woman from South Carolina arrived in St. Augustine. Lucy Abbott, described in her later years as a tiny woman with owl–like spectacles, played the real estate market admirably. She and her uncle, John Starke, rapidly developed land north of the Castillo de San Marcos. Miss Abbott is credited with building at least 10 homes on Water and Joyner streets, including the three–story structure known as Abbott Mansion. Deed records show her complicated land speculations from the 1870s into the 20th century.

While Miss Abbott was measuring lots and watching the walls of her houses rise, other women seeking work were finding life less comfortable. According to the *Florida State Gazetteer* of 1883, the major field of employment for women at that time was handicrafting palmetto hats and bags or running boarding houses. In addition to the women mentioned above, Mrs. Hamilton ran the Benedict House, Mrs. John T. Edwards was the proprietress of Edward House, Mrs. J. V. Hernandez operated the Hernandez House, and Mrs. T. F. House managed the Sunnyside Hotel.

Women continued operating boarding houses into the 20th century but, fortunately a wider selection of occupations slowly became available. As early as 1897, Miss S. A. Winslow was earning a living as a chiropodist and manicurist. By 1899 women were proprietors of stores, frequently curiosity shops, and many entered the teaching profession. The tobacco industry was also open to women as some are listed as cigar makers. Dr. Mary Payne is the only female physician listed at the turn of the century. As the Flagler era began, the fashion conscious life–style of winter residents and wealthy St. Augustine residents created opportunities in the clothing field. Before the turn of the century, the millinery business had been dominated by Mrs. W. B. Crocker. By the early 1900s, more local women were attempting the trade. Two dressmakers from Atlanta, Georgia, Martha (Mattie) Lumstead and Mrs. Marie A. Spencer, paved the way for St. Augustine women seeking employment in that field.

It was during the late 1800s and early 1900s that men and women became increasingly aware of the changing role of women in the community. An editorial in *Tatler*, St. Augustine's society newspaper, deliberates female employment. After a shaky introduction stating, "...women's invasion of the commercial, professional, and labor world has a serious side not always pleasant to contemplate," the author writes, "when the millennium arrives women will have no occasion to work. Each woman will be properly mated and preside over a happy home." The author then asserted that "In selecting a (woman) lawyer or physician the question of ability should be considered. A woman may be as competent, as learned, and as experienced but be barred by sex." The *Tatler* article continued by recognizing the number of times women wrote editorial pages, law cases, even sermons, which were presented by husbands or employers who received the credit. The closing statement of the editorial delivers the message with a punch. "Make ability the standard, not sex, and the vexed question will be solved." It was a bold statement for 1900 and even more consequential when one considers the author was probably a woman, Anna Marcotte, the proprietor and editor of *Tatler*.

In 1904 a woman's name appeared for the first time in a popular new profession—photography. Helen E. Hall took her place with the other shutter bugs whose studios crowded St. George Street.

However, it was the teaching profession which attracted the largest number of working women, including the three Shorter sisters Maude, Effy, and May. All three women lived at *63 Orange Street*, where their mother ran a boarding house. Evelyn Hamblen appeared in the 1904 directory as a teacher. Her later career included chairing the St. Johns County Board of Public Instruction and a school now commemorates her fine abilities as an educator. In the early decades of the 20th century many familiar names began to appear in the field of education including Gertrude Speissegger, Laura Hawkins, Agnes Coughlin, Aileen Cooper, Margaret Gibbs, Christian Bonfield, and Mabel Hersey. In addition to teaching, several women became principals: Maude Shorter at the St. Augustine Junior High School and Rosemary Ringo at Fullerwood. Other principals during this era included Mabel Hersey, Minnie Pooser, Madge Turner, Irene L. Williams, and Jessie Avril. For a time Myrtie W. Felkel served as principal of the private Palm Row School. However, when her husband died, she managed the family insurance business. Careers in journalism also became available to women in the early 1900s. Nina Hawkins began a long career as editor of the *St. Augustine Evening Record* in the 1920s. By the 1920s and 1930s, there were several female reporters including Phyllis Usina, Lucille Tervin, and Adelaide Sanchez.

As early as 1914, African–American women were creating new career paths. Ella K. Quinn practiced as an osteopath in the Jefferson Theatre Building. Ida B. Peronneau was a chiropodist and then matron at the St. Johns County Infirmary. Carrie Macon owned and operated a successful beauty shop on St. George Street for many years.

During the 1920s, careers for women expanded. Rebecca Botkowsky was advertising manager of the Record Company. Delia M. Beardsley was supervisor of the East Coast Hospital. Emily L. Wilson held the position of historian and librarian of the St. Augustine Historical Society during the 1920s and 1930s. Two women found careers in medicine: Dr. Roberta T. Graham, chiropractor, and Dr. Mary Lapham, listed as a physician. It was in the 1920s that Lila M. Snow, widow of W. Wallace Snow, assumed the responsibility for the real estate and insurance business her husband established. Rosalie Pomar, the widow of Anthony V., became proprietor of the St. George Electric Company. Clerical fields opened during the 1920s as women entered new occupations as bookkeepers, notaries, real estate brokers, and stenographers.

Although the city directory was invaluable in compiling a list of names, addresses, and occupations, it could not supply the flavor of human experience. Newspaper articles and oral legends helped add color to some of the names of the city's famous and infamous women.

Louella Day McConnell resided at *155 Magnolia Street.* "Diamond Lil," as she was sometimes called, was probably St. Augustine's most colorful female character. Reputedly educated as a physician, this unusual woman traveled to the Klondike where she made her fortune. She found her way to St. Augustine around 1900 flashing a wad of bills and a diamond in her front tooth. She fabricated stories about Ponce de Leon's discovery of the "Fountain of Youth" and continued to amuse and appall St. Augustine residents until her death in 1927.

The literary contributions of Edith Taylor Pope and part–time city resident, Marjorie Kinnan Rawlings far surpassed the average expectations of any person of the city. Mrs. Pope, daughter of Senator A. M. Taylor and wife of Senator Verle Pope, left her mark through such novels as *Colcorton*. Marjorie Kinnan Rawlings wrote about Florida from her home in Cross Creek and received a Pulitzer Prize for her work. She spent much of her time with her husband, Norton Baskin, assisting in the operation of the Castle Warden Hotel which he owned.,

Although the emphasis in the above section has been on the period ending in 1930, as is the case throughout the state and the nation, women are now involved in politics, law, medicine, and industry as well as continuing to distinguish themselves in careers in education, art, music, and the businesses centered in the Ancient City.

"Ladies Entrance," etching by Otto Bacher, 1890
Ponce de León Hotel

Glossary
of
Terms

ASHLAR: Squared hewn stone or scoring (drawing lines in building material to give the appearance of square stones.

BALUSTER: The small post that supports a railing. A series of these is called a balustrade.

CAPITALS: The uppermost part of a column, pillar, or pilaster. The classical orders are Doric, Ionic, and Corinthian increasing from simple to elaborate.

CARPENTER GOTHIC: An American version of the Gothic revival which includes sawn wood ornamentation "gingerbread" of the barge boards and eaves of a roof.

CHAMFERED POSTS: Porch posts cut vertically to create four flat sides on a round column.

CORBEL: A bracket or block projection from the face of a wall that generally supports a cornice, beam, or arch.

COQUINA: A native shellstone found primarily on Anastasia Island and quarried during colonial days for building the Castillo de San Marcos and other buildings.

CROWSTEPPED GABLES: A roof design resembling stair steps.

CUPOLA: A small dome on a roof.

DORMER: A vertically set window on a sloping roof.

FAN LIGHT: A semi-circular window over a door or window with radiating bars or tracery in the form of an open fan.

FINIAL: An ornament rising above a gable or spire.

GABLE: The triangular part of an exterior wall created by the angle of a pitched roof.

GINGERBREAD: See Carpenter Gothic.

GOTHIC: A term referring to a style of architecture using pointed arches and steep roofs.

HIP ROOF: A roof with sloping ends and sides and no gable.

HORNWORK (HORNABEQUE): An earthenwork defense line constructed in 1719 having a curtain and two half-bastions creating a look resembling the projecting horns of a bull.

JIG-SAWN BRACKETS: Projections from the face of a building supporting a cornice or ornamental feature which have been sawed to create a design. The feature was used extensively in Victorian house styles and was often referred to as "gingerbread."

LOGGIA: An open, roofed area, usually with arches, opening onto a courtyard.

MANSARD ROOF: The classic mansard roof has steep sides broken by dormer windows. It is named after the French architect, Francois Mansart, and was a prominent feature of the Second Empire style in the mid-19th century.

MEDITERRANEAN REVIVAL: An architectural style associated with the Florida boom of the 1920s. Hallmarks of the style include clay tile roofs or cornices, stucco finish, and the use of an arch motif on windows, doors, and porches. Casement and fanlight windows are found along with ornamental ironwork for window grilles and balconets.

MIL Y QUINIENTAS: This Spanish term literally means 1,500 referring to 1,500 varas (Spanish yards). It signifies the 3/4 mile area outside the defense line cleared of foliage which could hide an approaching enemy. It was created during the second Spanish period.

MOORISH REVIVAL: An architectural style introduced in St. Augustine in the 1880s. It included poured concrete walls and a flat roof with a parapet decorated with cast concrete ornamentation, giving the appearance of a "castle."

NEO-CLASSICAL: Refers to a revival of the early Greek and Roman form of architecture.

PEDIMENT: A triangular gable above a door, window, or entablature (the upper part of column and capital).

PENDANT: A hanging ornament on roofs and ceilings as a decorative feature of Gothic Revival architecture.

PIAZZA: An open public place surrounded by buildings.

PILASTER: A rectangular column projecting from a wall rather than free-standing.

PORTICO: An open entrance to a building supported by columns.

QUEEN ANNE STYLE: See Victorian.

SANBORN FIRE INSURANCE MAPS: Early insurance maps indicating the location, configuration, size, and building materials of buildings within the city limits.

SPANISH REVIVAL ARCHITECTURE: An architectural style drawing from Spanish architecture in the period after the Moors were expelled from the country. Elements include poured concrete walls, clay tile roofs, towers, rounded arches, and extensive terra cotta ornamentation.

TABBY: A building material made from a mixture of lime, shell, sand, and water.

TESSELLATE: To inlay, lay out, or pave with small square blocks in a mosaic-like pattern.

TUSCAN: Referring to the classic order of architecture characterized by unfluted columns with a ring-like capital and frieze similar to the Doric style.

VENITIAN RENAISSANCE REVIVAL: An architectural style referring to Venetian influence to include poured concrete walls, clay tile roofs, and extensive terra cotta ornamentation that is white and old-gold in color rather than red.

VERNACULAR: Wooden buildings constructed in St. Auugstine before 1930 that do not fall into any specific architectural category are listed as "frame vernacular."

VICTORIAN: The term used to cover various kinds of houses and public buildings built during the reign of Queen Victoria (1837-1901) and into the 20th century. The most elaborate of the massive buildings was the Queen Anne style using decorative features including a variety of sidings, an irregular plan, ornamental brickworks on chimneys, and the use of towers and turrets as well as porches and bay windows.

Author's Comment

It has been a decade since the Historic St. Auugstine Preservation Board completed its hallmark survey. Home owners and researchers frequently turn to the site files for information about historic and architecturally significant buildings and sites. We are fortunate to have that information, but what has been learned from it?

America's First City has approximately 40 colonial and Territorial buildings remaining. We are proud of our magnificent Spanish and Venetian Renaissanced and Moorish Revival buildings as well as the elegant Victgorian homes located throughout the city's neighborhoods. We can look with pride at the heritage derived from our first Spanish period families, the Solano(a), Sanchez, and Arsian-Alverez-Gonzales families and the numerous Minorcan and Greek descendants of the New Smyrna colony.

However, many buildings included in the survey have been sadly neglected. Although some homes along Water Street in the Abbott Tract have been beautifully maintained, it is disappointing to see the deterioration of those whose dignity has been lost in one short decade. It is a pleasure to see the maintenance and restoration of buildings in Lighthouse Park, including the new lighthouse keepers' house and a shame to look at those magnificent structures that lack the care their heritage should insure. A look at Lincolnville highlights the situation. Some of the Victorian homes shine; however, one historic street is dotted with vacant buildings. The Lincolnville Restoration Committee is committed to improving the situation.

If we are to understand and sustain our heritage, we must also protect its future. The Historic St. Augustine Preservation Board's goals can only accomplish part of the task. Our community as well as those across the nation, must continue to support and maintain our shared historic and architectural heritage. St. Augustine, America's First City, represents the vanguard of that quest.

Photographic
Credits

Thank you for selecting *America's First City, St. Augustine's Historic Neighborhoods*. Other books published and/or distributed by Tailored Tours Publications are described below.

An Uncommon Guide to Florida, A Resident's Guide to the Real Florida. The glove compartment travel companion for residents, newcomers, and tourists. With over 1,000 activities, presented as part of 24 tours, travelers will find new and "uncommon" locations while exploring the state's past, present, and future. A 224 page guide book, with over 80 photographs and illustrations, the book outlines special things to do and see for all age groups.
Price: $12.95

Florida Atlas & Gazetteer. A unique atlas that maps Florida's back roads and serves as an excellent companion to An Uncommon Guide to Florida. The maps show an enormous variety of geographic features and make it "almost" impossible to lose your way. Full color maps: scale of 1" to 2.3 miles, 103 maps, 128 pages, DeLorme. Price $14.95

Accidental Hostess, Florida's Answer to Coping with Constant Company. Written in Florida, by Floridians who are entertaining in Florida. A light-hearted book that is helpful and hilarious. Suggestions cover visits from family, dear friends, drop ins, and Spring Breakers. Includes menus and over 100 recipes, 146 pages. Price: $9.95

An Uncommon Guide to North Carolina: A Tar Heel's Travel Companion. Travel the Great Smokeys to the Outer Banks, and through the rest of the state with this illustrated glove compartment guide. A must for North Carolina visitors and residents. Price: $12.95

North Carolina Atlas & Gazetteer. Another in the series of unique atlases. Maps the state's highways, byways, and back roads. A perfect companion volume to An Uncommon Guide to North Carolina. DeLorme. Price: 14.95

These titles can be purchased through your bookseller, or can be ordered from Tailored Tours Publications, Box 22861, Lake Buena Vista, FL 32830 for the price of the book plus $2 per title to cover tax, shipping, and handling.

Tailored Tours Publications is committed to developing fine regional, travel-related books. We would be pleased to hear from you concerning your comments regarding America's First City as well as your thoughts about other regional publications you feel would be of interest.

My comments are:

_____

_____

_____

_____

_____

☐ Check here if you would like to be added to our mailing list and please provide your name and address below.

_____

_____

_____

Please mail to:

Tailored Tours Publications, Inc.
Box 22861
Lake Buena Vista, FL 32830